THE HUNTER
in Pictures

By the author of

THE AMERICAN QUARTER HORSE IN PICTURES
THE MORGAN HORSE IN PICTURES
HORSEMAN'S ENCYCLOPEDIA
HORSES: THEIR SELECTION, CARE AND HANDLING
THE COMPLETE BOOK OF HORSES AND PONIES

Shown overleaf:

The Moore County Hounds of Southern Pines, North Carolina, hacking to the meet. The going is fast, the fences mostly timber and the country pretty well free of underbrush. There is no problem with boggy terrain or rough ground, large stones or narrow, winding trails. Thus a swift mount with a good mixture of Thoroughbred is suitable. From the left, 1st Whipper-in Mrs. W. O. Moss (also honorary secretary), Master and Huntsman W. O. Moss, 2nd Whipper-in Wiffi Smith, Field Master and Joint MFH Richard Webb.

Courtesy of Page Shamburger—Photo by Emerson Humphrey

Margaret Cabell Self

THE HUNTER in Pictures

MACRAE SMITH COMPANY
Philadelphia

ISBN: 0–8255–8237–7

Library of Congress Catalog Card Number 72:4380

Designed by William E. Lickfield

Manufactured in the United States of America

Published simultaneously in Canada by George J. McLeod, Limited, Toronto

7208

Foreword

THE HUNTER IN PICTURES presents a cross section of the type of hunter to be found not only in the hunting field but in the show ring as well. Since the type of country over which hounds and horses are expected to travel affects the choice of horse, this too is discussed, along with a brief history of hunting *per se.* I would like to thank all the many contributors of the pictures that make this book possible, and especially *The Maryland Horse,* whose editor, Mr. Snowden Carter, not only helped me to locate a great many but provided a number himself, including all those in the Steeplechases and Point-to-Points section.

MARGARET CABELL SELF

Contents

THE HUNTER
in Pictures

Part I

Hunting

There is no fixed date as to when hunting on horseback first became popular. Prehistoric man first hunted on foot in packs, some chasing the quarry while others waited to cut it off and surround it for the kill. The only object was to obtain food for the tribe.

Sometime later men discovered that a stone ax, thrown with accuracy, enabled the hunter to kill from a distance. As time went on other weapons such as the thrown spear and the bow and arrow came into use, and men could hunt alone.

Even with the help of these weapons, hunting on foot must have proved a real challenge. Think of the change when man, having learned to train the horse, started using him as a means of transport which enabled him to outrun the game he wished to pursue! Hittite pictures drawn two thousand years before Christ depict hunters using spears to kill all types of game, including lions, both while mounted and while being driven in a two-wheeled vehicle. Hunting became a sport.

Since these times, people have hunted for food and for sport in all parts of the world. In Greece, five centuries before Christ, Xenophon wrote three books on training horses for warfare, for pleasure and for hunting. Tapestries, paintings, stone tablets, decorations on ceramics and pottery and the like depict the hunts of Egyptians, Gauls, Romans, Persians, Chinese and other peoples. The Bible reports that Nimrod was a "famous hunter before the Lord." Quarries included the wild boar, lion, ostrich, fox, wolf and stag, the last being most popular. Sometimes dogs were used, sometimes not.

In the eighth century, St. Hubert became the patron saint of hunting among Christians, and during the Middle Ages people in all walks of life enjoyed the chase. The clergy, including abbesses, were particularly enthusiastic. A book called *Livre de Chasse,* written in 1387 by Gaston de Foix, discusses in detail the science of hunting.

Kings and nobles had their private packs, with the hunt servants wearing the livery of the owner. The earliest recorded pack kept for hunting in France was that of Louis XIII. In Italy at that time hunting was also much appreciated, especially by the court ladies. In Russia not only did the hunt servants wear special liveries but their horses were frequently matched in color, just as today hunt teams competing in shows are usually mounted on matched horses.

By the year 1739 hunting in the New World was well established, with packs in Montreal, Canada, Baltimore, Washington, D.C., and Virginia. The first formal hunt club founded in the United States was the Gloucester Foxhunting Club, founded in Philadelphia in 1766. However, the British Isles and Southern Ireland have always provided the best fox and stag hunting to be found anywhere on earth.

Even during wartime hunting was not forgotten. Knights and Crusaders, royalty and clergy, all took time off from the perils of battle to pursue whatever quarry was available. The Duke of Wellington is said to have been so foresighted as to have the earths stopped ahead of him (the foxes' burrows were blocked at night while they foraged, to prevent their going to ground the next day) so that he and his officers could have plenty of sport. And George Washington in his diaries tells of almost daily hunting even during his revolutionary campaigns.

During World War I, several British regiments kept hounds in France, and one pack got as far as Italy, while American troops both hunted and played polo at Coblenz.

The earliest-known painting of foxhounds with the hunt staff shows the Viscount Lowther's hounds leaving Fineshade Abbey, Northampton, England, in 1695. They were probably the first organized pack in the country. Their descendents were eventually bought by William the Good, First Earl of Lonsdale by the second creation. He inherited the Lowther estates and fortune from a distant cousin known as "Wicked Jimmy," who died without heirs. Practically every hound in England today dates back to this pack. Sir William was so devoted to his hounds that he hunted them for seven months of the year; then he spent a month trotting them the two hundred miles from Cottesmore, where he kenneled them, to Lowther Hall for the summer, and another month trotting them to Cottesmore again in the fall. He virtually initiated the science of their selective breeding, and the Cottesmore Hounds are still among the best known and finest in England.

WHY HUNT THE FOX?

The primary purpose of hunting the fox in England and in Ireland both yesterday and today is to keep the fox population down. Formerly the fox had wolf packs to keep him under control, but with the advent of civilization these vanished, and for centuries the fox has had no natural enemies. Yet foxes are predatory animals and, if allowed to become too numerous, can decimate the livestock of the countryside, raising havoc with the farmers' poultry and even attacking his newborn lambs.

If it is deemed necessary to exterminate the fox, it might be argued, why not do it with poison or firearms? The answer is not so simple. Poison is dangerous to other animals as well. To be killed with a gun, the fox must first be located and then induced to leave his burrow. Furthermore, a shot may only wound and not kill, dooming an animal to hours or even days of suffering.

The fox hunter believes that in pursuing the fox with a pack of hounds he is simply following nature's own method of control of the species, for he is substituting hounds for wolves, the animal's natural enemy. At the same time he is winning the approval of the farmer who wants to sleep soundly at night, knowing that his poultry and lambs are safe, and he is providing himself and his friends with a sport which, in the words of John Jorrocks, hero of the novel *Handley Cross,* is "The sport of kings and the image of war without its guilt and with only five and twenty percent of the danger."

SOME DIFFERENT HUNTING COUNTRIES

Hunting in England in the days of William the Good was very different from what it is today. The Leicestershire countryside was unfenced and undrained. A fox, once found, was hunted with slow determination, the Master of Foxhounds, Huntsman, Whippers-in and Members of the Field trotting along behind while the pack nosed the fox in and out of one covert after another. Horses that could gallop fast and jump boldly were not needed.

However, as the years passed, conditions changed. Fields were drained by digging ditches around them, the earth being thrown to the outside. Thus developed the famous "ditch and bank" jumps of England and Ireland, a type of obstacle unknown in the New World. Sometimes a low fence or guard rail was constructed on the edge of the ditch, to keep the cattle from falling in. As years went by the ditches became deeper and the banks higher. Often another ditch on the far side of the bank was put in to drain the adjoining field. Brush and thornbushes were encouraged to grow on the banks, both to prevent erosion and to further discourage the stock from escaping. Instead of ditches, thick thorn hedges were planted in country that did not need draining, and these served as fences to keep the stock confined. Other fences, known as "stake and bound" fences, were constructed also.

In Ireland, the soggiest of all hunting countries, the banks formed by digging the tremendously deep and wide drains have grown to such enormous heights that to attempt to "fly" them is suicide, for there is no way to determine what lies on the far side. So the sagacious equine Irish hunter approaches his obstacle slowly and judges the width of the ditch with great care, often coming to a standstill to do so. He then jumps deliberately but powerfully, landing either on top of the bank, if it is not over five or six feet high, or on its side, if it is higher. In the latter case he scrambles to the summit, takes a good look to see what lies before him, then sails into the air to land galloping.

In some parts of England and Ireland there are stone walls, often low and solid. The Irish horses treat them as banks, changing legs on top and landing amid a litter of falling or fallen rocks. Yet so skillful are they that they manage to step between the stones rather than on them. In Galway the walls are high and made of large stones balanced one upon the other. The crevices are not filled, and the whole gives a lacy effect. These the horses fly.

In certain parts of Ireland, especially in the stag-hunting country, the drains are very deep and very wide, too wide to be negotiated in one leap. There are no banks, the earth having been removed to make more pastureland. Here the horses have developed a still different technique. They gallop to the brink, stop, sit back on their haunches and slide a few feet down the sloping side, then spring across the chasm (which narrows as it deepens), land lightly on the far side and scramble to the top.

The Canadian country is rugged, with a good deal of timber. As in many parts of the United States, such as New England, panels are set into whatever type of fence is being used. Chicken coops, post-and-rails and stone walls with a wooden rider on top are the most common. In Canada tree roots are sometimes utilized, or great logs cut into short lengths and set on end.

There is no fox hunting in Mexico, but there is one pack of beagles which follows a drag. (In drag hunting, hounds that have been following a line made by dragging litter from a fox's bedding receive their reward in the form of meat when they run the "quarry" to ground.) The country is arid in the winter, stony and hilly, but because it is not fenced there are no real obstacles. However, the ground is so hard that it is more like concrete than earth, and it is unlikely that hunting as found in other countries will ever become very practical, though there are rumors that it is to be tried in the state of Guanajuato.

United States hunting country varies from the wide galloping fields of the South to the small, heavily wooded fields of New England. There are no drains, banks or thorn hedges. In New England stone walls predominate; in other parts of the country various types of wooden fencing are more common. Panels are often introduced, especially where the takeoff and landing must be selected carefully.

The type of country affects the type of hunting. In England, because the country is open and the coverts small and generally crossed with "rides" (trails), the foxhound is much more disciplined and more dominated in his work than is his American counterpart. The English have been breeding and training hounds for centuries, and the results are evident. In Ireland the same type of hound is used, but the hunting is freer and less formal. The "fields," meaning the number of riders, are small compared to those of England and the country less built up; hounds seldom have to be whipped off because the quarry has run into forbidden territory.

In the United States much of the country is impenetrable by a mounted rider. Hence hounds work a good deal on their own. Most are not as well disciplined as their English cousins, but they are large and very fast. In many sections the country has become so chopped up with building that fox hunting as such is no longer practical and drag hunting only is practiced. This also demands fast-going hounds. In other parts an overabundance of foxes and the presence of many deer have made ordinary fox hunting impractical except with exceptionally well-disciplined packs, and again drag hunting is popular.

Hunting with bloodhounds is little known, but the author

introduced this sport in New England thirty years ago. It is most suitable for areas where deer or other animals abound and the country is limited, and especially for pony clubs and riding schools. Only one or two hounds are used, which need not be kenneled but may be kept as pets. It is not necessary to lay a drag; instead, one or two riders take the part of the quarry and ride off while the hounds, hunt staff and field wait for five or ten minutes. When the minutes of grace are over, hounds are released. Uttering deep bell-like tones, they drop their noses to the ground and pick up the scent of the riders immediately, never losing the trail no matter how tricky the line as ridden by the human "foxes." Bloodhound hunting is an excellent and inexpensive sport, and allows young people to be introduced to the etiquette of the field as well as have a fine time.

For those who feel that fox hunting and following the harriers is bloodthirsty, stag hunting, as carried on in Ireland, is a marvelous sport. Stag so used are kept in kennels. On the day of the hunt a stag is "carted" (carried in a trailer or van) to the section of the country chosen for that day, released and given enough grace to permit him to get a good head start. Off he goes with a terrific bound. It takes a fast pack of hounds and fast-going horses to keep up, especially if the country is open. When he becomes tired of the chase, Sir Stag simply goes to the nearest river or lake and wades into it up to his chest. There he waits until the hunt catches up to him. The Huntsman calls off hounds, bundles the stag back into his vehicle, and he returns to his kennel having had a most enjoyable afternoon.

There is a long list of books on hunting, too long to give here, but I would like to mention again the novel by Robert Smith Surtees called *Handley Cross*, John Woodcock Graves's "John Peel" and John Masefield's "Reynard the Fox." Surely no hunting afficionado lives who is not familiar with these three.

1. Hunting in England with staghounds in the early 1800s. These belong to the Earl of Derby. From left to right: Lord Stanley; the Honorable E. Stanley; Jonathan Griffin, Huntsman, on Spanker (gray horse); and First Whipper-in on Noodle.

Painted by I. Barenger *Engraved by R. Woodman*
Courtesy of Mr. and Mrs. Ormond Wilcox
Photo by Bernard Kramer

2. Drain with guard rail. Original title, "Mr. Cooper and Pony." This is one of a series of sporting prints published in London by Lewis and Johnson in 1826.

Painted by J. Pollard *Engraved by C. Rosenberg*
Courtesy of Mr. and Mrs. Ormond Wilcox
Photo by Bernard Kramer

3. Here we see Mr. Seffert on Grimaldi, jumping the much feared five-barred gate and one of his companions as well. This is from the same series as the two previous pictures and the two that follow.

Courtesy of Mr. and Mrs. Ormond Wilcox
Photo by Bernard Kramer

4. Fording a stream. Notice the thorn fence in the background. The original title of this picture was "No joys can compare to the sports of the field." The gentleman in the foreground is Captain Becher, for whom the famous obstacle known as "Becher's Brook" on the Grand National Course was named.

Courtesy of Mr. and Mrs. Ormond Wilcox
Photo by Bernard Kramer

5. A drain and guard rail as seen from the landing side. This is Mr. Rice on Red-Deer taking the obstacle in the style of 1826.

Courtesy of Mr. and Mrs. Ormond Wilcox
Photo by Bernard Kramer

6. The famous Exmoor Hounds, a fine example of a modern English pack, moving off at the heels of the Master of Foxhounds (or MFH), Mr. Jack Hosegood. Notice the six-foot bank topped with an almost impenetrable hedge. Such an obstacle is known as a "bullfinch." Where the country is hunted frequently there may be gaps broken through the hedges, usually just barely large enough for horse and rider to push through. The latter's clothes and often his face may suffer from the encounter, but it is all taken simply as one of the joys of the chase!

Courtesy of The Maryland Horse *Photo by John Tarlton*

7. The Moore County Hounds of Southern Pines, North Carolina, hacking to the meet. In this country the going is fast: the fences mostly timber, the coverts usually pine forests with very little underbrush. There are no problems such as boggy terrain or rough, narrow, stony trails. Thus a swift, bold mount with a goodly mixture of Thoroughbred is suitable. (In Canada, for example, a heavier type of horse is needed.) From the left: First Whipper-in Mrs. W. O. Moss (she is also the honorary secretary of the hunt), Master and Huntsman W. O. Moss, Second Whipper-in Wiffi Smith; Field Master and Joint MFH Richard Webb.

Courtesy of Page Shamburger *Photo by Emerson Humphrey*

8. Mr. Sherman Haight's Litchfield County Hounds of Litchfield, Connecticut. This is typical New England country, wooded, stony, with small open fields and many streams, which must be forded. MFH Sherman Haight, Jr., is on the left with Field Master Lloyd Almiral beside him. First Whipper-in Peggy Haight on the gray, together with the Second Whipper-in, keep hounds moving, while a member of the field brings up at the rear.

Courtesy of Mrs. Reginald Francklyn

9. Beagles, the smallest of the hound breeds, whose quarry is rabbits, are usually hunted on foot. Here we see Philip Crowe with his beagle pack in New Canaan, Connecticut. This picture was taken about 1935 by Sydney B Self, Jr.

10. However, Patrick Tritton has a pack of beagles which he uses for drag hunting in Mexico, hunt staff and field all being mounted. In this picture, which gives a good idea of the rocky, arid, hilly country on the central plateau, Harold Black (center foreground), owner of the Escuela Ecuestre, a riding establishment, watches closely as hounds search out the scent. The Master is on the right.

Photo by Lois Hobart

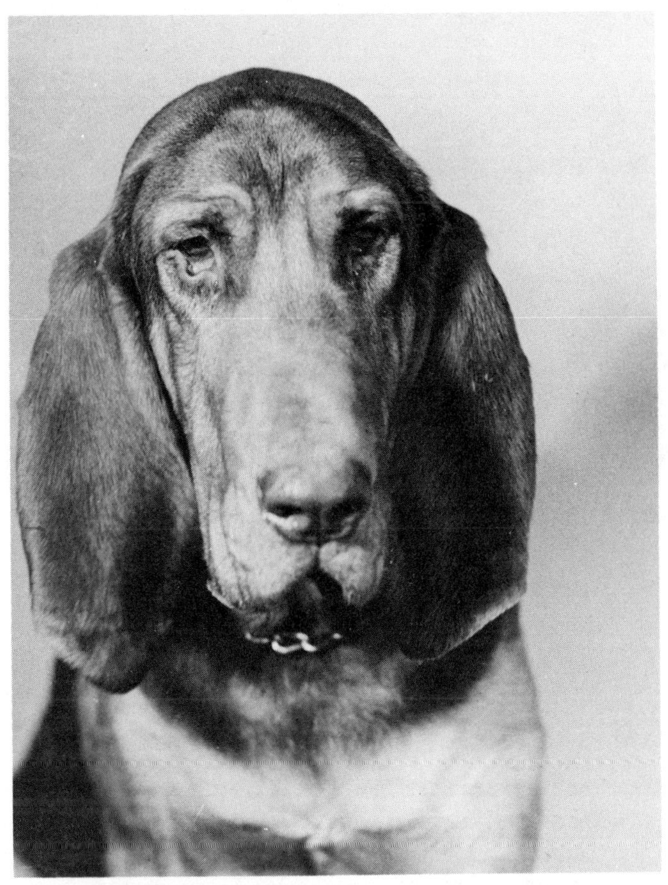

11. Rip was a magnificent specimen of a bloodhound, with his domed head, long ears, wrinkles and look of wisdom. Rip could follow the scent of a rider through snow, stream or dry pasture. He often ran several hundred yards downwind, yet knew at once when the quarry had changed direction. His voice was deep and belltoned. He gave tongue continuously and was never known to lose the line or be distracted by deer or the crossing of the original line by as many as twenty other riders.

Photo by Sydney B. Self, Jr.

12. Like most innovations, driving tandem, as shown here, came from necessity. Before the days of horse vans and trains equipped to transport horses, afficionados of the chase often had to hack ten or more miles to the meet. To ride this distance on a horse that would then be expected to gallop all day across rough country would have put too great a strain on him. Hence the idea of the tandem. The hunter was placed in the lead where he need not exert himself unduly, since on the horse between the shafts, the wheeler, rests the burden of pulling the weight of the cart on the level and up steep grades, and of sitting back on the breeching on downhill grades to prevent the vehicle from running him down. "Barbary packs" were common. In these packs the hounds were not owned by a specific establishment, being trained and kenneled together; rather they consisted of animals belonging to different owners which were kept by their various masters and brought together the day of the meet only. In such cases driving tandem served a second purpose. The high, rather heavy two-wheeled vehicle used, known as a "dog cart," had an enclosed space under the driver's seat in which several hounds could be accommodated. Thus the rider could arrive at the covert side having tired neither himself nor his hunter and with his own hounds also fresh and ready to go. These are two of the Liseter Hall Farm Welsh ponies, Liseter Brilliant and Liseter Bright Crocus. Both are hunting ponies and have proved their worth in the show ring and in the field.

Courtesy of Mrs. J. Austin du Pont *Photo by Tarrance*

13. Some idea of the type of establishment needed to maintain a pack of hounds and the necessary staff, with their mounts, may be realized on viewing this aerial picture of the kennels of the Moore County Hounds at Mile-Away Farms in Southern Pines, North Carolina. Notice the sand ring for exercising and training the hunt staff horses; the Hitchcock pen in the center, used for free schooling; and the kennels with their adjacent runs containing raised benches. There are several stables and barns and a cottage as well. A track encircles the largest part of the area, permitting the exercising and schooling of young horses both at the trot and the gallop without having to expose them to the excitement of open country until they are ready for it. This track can also be used in the education of the "young entry" (hounds in their first year of training).

Courtesy of Page Shamburger

14. Hunting has many traditions and ceremonies that date back to early times. Among these is the Blessing of the Hounds, which takes place annually at the beginning of the season and is intended to ensure the health and safety of the pack and to guarantee many successful and fast runs. These are the Green Spring Valley Hounds being blessed at St. John's Church in Glyndon, Maryland.

Courtesy of The Maryland Horse *"Jacques Photography"*

15. Moore County Hounds in full cry on a burning scent —that is, running fast over open country on a fresh strong trail.

Courtesy of Page Shamburger

16. A momentary check as the Moore County Hounds negotiate a board fence on the hunter trail course. The Master, W. O. Moss, mounted on Carry On, is in the foreground. Mrs. Moss, First Whipper-in, is seen jumping the fence on Dark Victory.

Courtesy of Page Shamburger

17. The rugged country of Canada demands a horse of power and substance and hounds that can penetrate heavily wooded areas, such as appear here in the background, nosing out the fox and bringing him into the open without the help of the hunt staff. The horse facing the camera in the center is Sundance, a splendid example of the Canadian Half-bred who takes his spirit and speed from his Thoroughbred sire and his size, substance and staying power from his draft ancestry. Notice also the sturdy quarters of the Master's horse, whose back is toward the camera. They are reminiscent of the powerful Irish hunter, which can be belly deep in bog and hoist himself out without injuring his tendons.

Courtesy of Col. and Mrs. Arthur McKibbon

18. In England, where earths are stopped, kills are common. Not so in the United States, where the fox has about a 99 percent chance of escaping to run again another day. Here we see a kill at Paddock, Jr., in South Carolina, owned by Mrs. Gardiner Fiske. Mrs. Moss, First Whipper-in for the Moore County Hounds, is shown in the left foreground on her Halfbred stallion Battlewick. She whipped off this horse through his seventeenth year. As of 1971, he was twenty-five years old, well and still catching his mares. Among his currently famous get are Spindletop Showdown, Conformation Horse of 1970, Li-Ke, Working Hunter Champion of 1970, and Crag's Corner, Virginia top-scoring hunter of that year.

Courtesy of Page Shamburger

Part II

Breeds and Types

In practically every breed of horse (with the exception of the Tennessee Walking Horse and the Five-gaited American Saddler) we find some animals that are used and shown successfully as hunters. Even more popular are the various crossbreeds. And we often find exceptionally good field hunters whose breeding is undefined or traces back to so many different bloodlines that one cannot classify the animal. The reason for the wide variety of horses used for hunting is the wide variety of country (both the terrain and the obstacles) over which they hunt and the equally wide variety of riders.

A hunter is not chosen only for the specific purpose (except, of course, those which are picked for showing and must only please the judges), he is chosen because he suits the needs of the buyer. A Master of Foxhounds, Huntsman or Whipper-in will need a bold animal that is easily controlled and unafraid of any type of fence, one that can be trusted to keep his feet out of the way of hounds and is prepared to go into the most unprepossessing-looking covert, get out the hounds that are lingering or are tempted by a false scent and, having gotten out these malingerers, catch up to the pack. Many young people want a gay animal that will take anything and take it well, and if he puts in a few bucks now and again it just gives them the opportunity to show off their horsemanship. An experienced rider, interested in watching hounds work, wants a horse that will carry him safely over the country, stand quietly while he listens to the voices of the distant pack, stay back without fussing, wait his turn at a panel or give a lead to more reluctant and unexperienced animals, and be willing to leave the other riders and take his own line when necessary.

It goes without saying that everyone wants an animal that will stay sound. This means that he must be chosen with an eye to the weight of the rider and the type of country. It would be suicide to take a finely bred hunter champion from Virginia, let us say, and expect him to hunt successfully in County Limerick, Ireland. The heavy going would have him lame after the first or second run. He would probably not even get as far as a second run for, being unprepared for the hazardous ditches that lie on the far side of many banks and walls, most likely he would come a cropper in the first such obstacle he met with. Similarly, an Irish-bred and -trained hunter would never face the timber that the Virginia hunter flies without hesitation.

All good hunters must have manners. A horse that won't stand quietly to be mounted or to hold back a gate, a horse that is champing at his bit and doing a miniature *passage* every time he has to wait for his turn at a panel or that shakes his head and is restless at a check when all are listening for the welcome sounds that tell that the fox has gone away with hounds well and truly on his scent, a horse that lets fly at another horse when he is crowded or, worst sin of all, kicks or steps on a hound, is not going to be popular with the MFH, with the field or with his own rider.

A field hunter must also have stamina and must be able to stand after a fast run without running the risk of a chill. One that is going to hunt in New England or Canada will need heavy, dense bone, strong hocks and tendons that are not easily pulled by heavy going, for in these countries the fields are small and the ground often either boggy or hard and stony, but he will not need as much speed as will the hunter used in more open country.

And so it is easy to see why a person in search of a hunter that will carry him through a season is more interested in performance, manners and stamina than he is in beauty or bloodlines. The owner of a conformation show hunter, on the other hand, must take looks, style and "bloom" into consideration as well. And while the working show hunter may have some blemishes not permitted in the conformation horse, his looks will count too. Way of going, which includes evenness of stride, pace, smoothness in jumping and the like, is something to be considered in all types of hunters, whether for show or field work, but for the latter the rider will perhaps be more interested in knowing if his mount can get him out of a sticky situation safely than he is in whether he always takes the obstacles in stride. In the following pages we will examine various hunters that have made names for themselves, either in the field or in the hunter division of the show ring, or have proved themselves to be successful dams or sires of hunter.

Thoroughbred Hunters

19. **Night Season** (This Evening–Beverly Blue), foaled in 1962, stands 16:2 hands and is a fine example of a Thoroughbred stallion suitable to beget hunters both for field and show. He has been successful on grade as well as registered mares. He is the sire of the multiple stakes winner Burglary (seventeen races; $105,000) and full brother to the hunter champions Blue Hour and Quo Warranto. His get inherit his intelligence, good looks, sturdy build and dense bone, qualities that promise success in the field or show ring and a safe return after a fast run over difficult country.

Courtesy of Blackacre Farm *Photo by Chris Christenson, Jr.*

20. **Blue Hour,** #630018, here a yearling filly Thoroughbred also by This Evening out of Beverly Blue, presents a fine portrait of a young hunter in the making. At this age she stood 15:2 hands; she later matured just under 17 hands. She was bred by Mrs. T. E. Pittenger of Blackacre Farm, Peninsula, Ohio.

Courtesy of Blackacre Farm *Photo by Chris Christenson, Jr.*

21. **Tucker,** a splendid young Thoroughbred hunter, is here being shown in Rhode Island by Link Chaffee. His calmness and good form promise well for his future career either in the field or in the show ring.

Photo by Colin H. Brearley

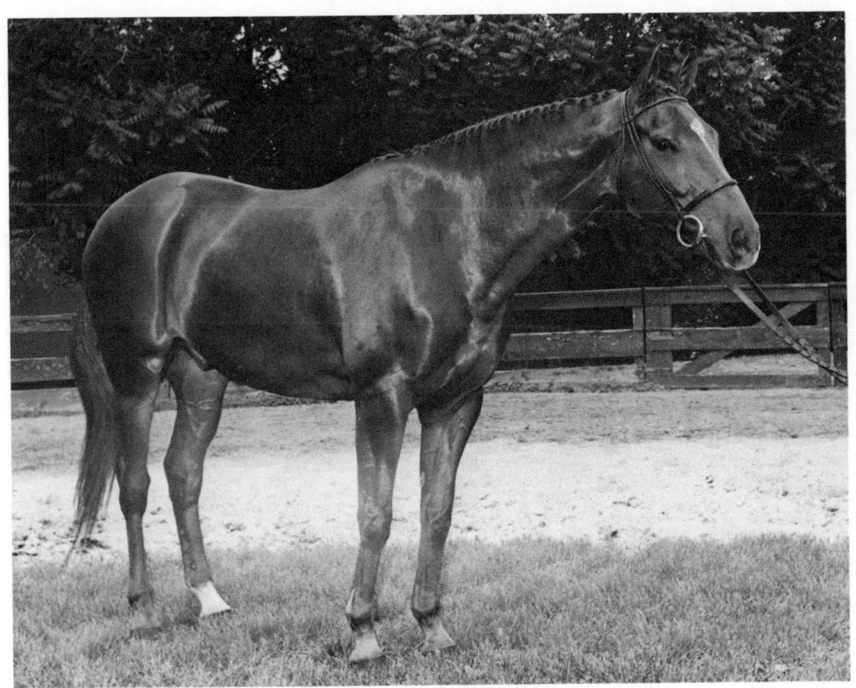

22. **Bound-to-Be,** a Thoroughbred chestnut gelding, was Green Conformation Champion at the Sewickley Hunt Horse Show in Sewickley, Pennsylvania, in 1971. He is owned and shown by Miss Carol Shepard, trained by J. V. Frohm.

Courtesy of Miss Carol Shepard *Photo by Don Parker*

23. **Quo Warranto,** Thoroughbred Hunter Conformation Champion, also Amateur Owner Champion, 1970, Syracuse Chapter, Professional Horsemen's Association, is another of Miss Shepard's fine horses that was trained by Jack Frohm.

Courtesy of Miss Carol Shepard *Photo by Robert A. Heinold*

24. Thoroughbred hunter mares and foal in pasture. These mares are excellent examples of the type of brood mare used to produce hunter and show prospects. The gray is **I'm Keen** of the Chance Play line. She competed in Combined Training events before her retirement in 1950. The other mare is **Esterette,** #607340, by Fight-a-Little out of Ethelm by Golden Vein, with the four-month-old foal **Burglary,** #660278, at heel. The latter is by Night Season (see Fig. 19) and developed into an outstanding stakes winner.

Courtesy of Blackacre Farm.

American Saddlebred Hunters

There have been many American Saddlers of the three-gaited division that have made their names as both hunters and jumpers. Since the breed is derived directly from the Thoroughbred this is not surprising, their sensitivity, good dispositions and flexibility making them a delight to ride. They need the light hands of the experienced rider and are more suitable to be used in open country where the going is fast than in trappy country—country with such unexpected terrain as boggy spots or sharp turns—where the going is heavy.

Five-gaited animals are not often chosen to be developed as hunters or jumpers because of the possibility of their coming into a fence on a rack. However, the author hunted a five-gaited gelding for years, taught jumping on him and, because he was so smooth and so willing, assigned him to riders who might be slightly handicapped by such things as an arm in a sling! He lived and worked through his twenty-fifth year and never fell over a jump.

25. **Poetry in Motion,** #62436, a registered saddle-bred mare by Denmark's Bourbon Genius out of Warioto on Parade, is pictured here as ridden by Lt. Col. Guy Wathen, a British liaison officer at Fort Knox, Kentucky. The obstacle is five and a half feet, and Poetry in Motion fully lives up to her name, for she seemingly floats over it with no effort. This breed is also very popular for dressage, Col. Hiram Tuttle being extremely interested in them. One of his mares, American Beauty Rose, was shown in exhibition at Madison Square Garden with the Colonel using silk threads as reins.

Courtesy of Mr. Charles J. Cronin, Jr. *Photo by Hank Cohen*

26. **Rhythm Jet,** #44150, is a registered American Saddle Horse gelding by Rhythm Command out of Little Rose, she by Mountain Peavine. This royally bred gelding, hunting regularly with the Old Chatham Hounds in the trappy New England country, is the exception that proves the rule. He is shown here with his owner, Laine Wenhorf, taking a typical New England obstacle, a low wall with a timber rider.

Courtesy of Mrs. R. B. Taylor *Photo by Lees Studio*

Arabian Hunters

The Arabian is not usually thought of as making a good hunter because as a breed they are small and lightly put together, nor is jumping bred into them as with some other breeds. However, it must be remembered that the Arabian has many characteristics that qualify him for hunting. His respiratory system is unequaled; his dense bone and strong feet make him able to stay sound when more delicate horses will go lame; his disposition is ideal and though he is very sensitive he responds well under experienced and educated hands. Too, it must be remembered that all Thoroughbreds, and through them practically all light horses, trace back to the three original Arabian sires, the Byerly Turk, the Godolphin Barb and the Darley Arabian. These three stallions were imported into England from Arabia between the years 1690 and 1725 to be bred with the native mares for the express purpose of producing hunters and racehorses.

27. **Aazrak,** #10821, an Arabian stallion, 14:2½ (by Aarat out of Aazkara), has certainly had one of the most remarkable careers ever recorded. He started as a pony or lead horse at the track, where his duty was to escort the more nervous Thoroughbreds from the assembly ring to the starting gate. An untrustworthy track boy mishandled him to the extent that he first developed splints and then became foundered from too much galloping on gravel paths without being correctly warmed up or cooled out. He then became a tease stallion and was used to test mares to see whether or not they were ready to be bred. In this capacity he banged up his knees and sustained wire cuts, scars on both hind fetlocks, and boggy hocks. Later in his career he managed to injure a nerve in one front leg, which kept him out of the show ring and off the hunt field for several seasons. In spite of all these misfortunes, between the age of four (when Mrs.

James McKay took over his training) to the age of fifteen he accomplished the following: He won innumerable ribbons in Hunter, Jumper, English Pleasure, Western Pleasure, Dressage, Pole Bending, Hunter Hack, Stock Horse, Trail Horse and Harness classes. He qualified for national championships and won the New Jersey High Score Award. He was Reserve Champion on one of the 50-Mile Trail Ride competitions. He hunted regularly with the Elkridge-Harford Hounds in Maryland and, although his mouth never quite recovered from the abuse it received under the hands of the track boy, his manners are impeccable and he will take any type of obstacle without excitement. In fact, he often has to give a lead to more nervous hunters much larger than he.

In the stable as well as in the hunt field his calm disposition and his dominance over the other animals make him invaluable, for by example and by that subtle system, undecipherable by man, by which horses communicate with each other, he will quiet the most difficult ones and give confidence to the most afraid. He recently acted as foster father to an orphaned foal that none of the mares and geldings would accept and that was slowly fading away from sheer despondency.

In addition to his showing, hunting and other achievements he is a most prepotent sire, passing along all his good characteristics and his jumping ability. So let all horse lovers say "Hats off!" to Aazrak, a true Cinderella of a horse who, despite a very bad beginning, is finishing as a star.

Courtesy of Mrs. James McKay *Photo by Tarrance*

Morgan Hunters

Since the Morgan is one of the most versatile of horses, it is not surprising to find Morgans in the hunt field and in the show ring. Not all have jumping ability and not all are fleet, but their dispositions and their sturdiness make them especially valuable for the rider who is not interested in excitement, doesn't want to have to worry about his horse and does want something that will keep him out of trouble. After all, Justin Morgan, Foundation Sire from whom every registered Morgan is descended, was noted for his dexterity over obstacles, and if he was never hunted one must remember that there *were* no hunts in Vermont in his day.

28. **Devan Marsh Hawk,** #12590, by Devan Duke out of Devan Dimglow, is a fine example of a Morgan stallion trained as a hunter. His get have been outstanding on the track, in the hunt field and in the show ring. He is strongly line bred and traces back to the U.S. Morgan Horse Farm stallion Mansfield, one of the stallions introduced at the turn of the century to impart size and a higher wither to the original Morgan stock.

Courtesy of Blackacre Farm

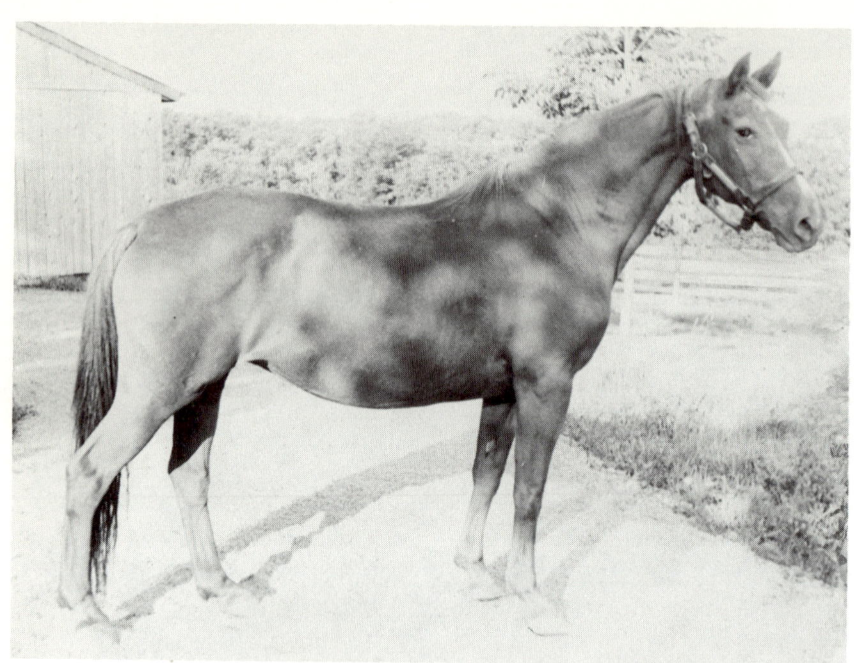

29. **Tippy-Dee,** #06510, a chestnut Morgan mare foaled in 1944, is by the U.S. stallion Hawk Jim out of Tippy-Tin, a mare bred by the U.S. Department of Agriculture. She is only eight generations removed from Justin Morgan, founder of the breed. This picture of Tippy-Dee was taken on her twenty-fifth birthday at Blackacre Farm, Peninsula, Ohio. This farm is owned by Mr. and Mrs. T. E. Pittenger, Jr. The Pittengers breed for beauty, soundness, versatility and disposition.

Courtesy of Blackacre Farm

30. **Debt,** #012790, and **Detinue,** #013549, each by Devan Marsh Hawk out of Tippy-Dee. Both these mares have shown successfully in hunt classes.

Courtesy of Blackacre Farm

31. Here is Detinue winning her class at the 1968 Hudson Kiwanis Show.

Courtesy of Blackacre Farm *Photo by Leslie Howard*

Quarter Horse Hunters

The Quarter Horse is also one of the most versatile of horses. Descended from Thoroughbred stock crossed with local Indian ponies of the South, it was developed through selective breeding and the introduction of other bloodlines for the purpose of getting off to a fast start and keeping up speed over a quarter-mile straight track. He is sometimes called "the horse that can run faster than anything else for as long as he can hold his breath." When Thoroughbred tracks were built in the South, quarter horses drifted west, where they were used extensively as stock horses. Not only their speed but their agility in stopping, starting and turning, their intelligence, fantastic balance, stamina and docility made them invaluable on the ranch and today makes them tops in such Western competitions as Stock Horses, Roping Horses and Cutting Horses. Not all quarter horses show aptitude for jumping, but many do and their strength and agility is as useful over the fences and in the field as it was in the old days on the quarter tracks and on the ranch.

32. **Kontiki,** a grade Quarter Horse gelding, 14:2, five years old, being shown in the large division of a Pony Hunter class at the Fort Meade Hunt Club in 1970 by his trainer, Joanie Lyons. Miss Lyons, who is fourteen years old, acquired him as a green broke two-year-old, trained him herself and showed him as a hunter. He is very gentle, jumps five feet easily and placed fourth in the Maryland Green Pony Hunter Standings for the year 1970.

Courtesy of Mr. Richard Marsh *Photo by Wilson Holder*

33. **Major Janney** is a registered Quarter Horse that started his career as a roping horse. He was the winner of many senior and junior hunter ribbons in 1970 in Colorado. He was trained by Mr. and Mrs. Janney with some supervision by Hans Moeller and is shown here, with Mrs. Janney up, negotiating the last of a group of cavaletti jumps set on 21-foot stride to increase the arc and use of his back in jumping.

Courtesy of St. Finnbarr Farm

Holsteiners

In Germany one of the most popular breeds for jumpers and three-day horses (those who compete in three-day events: dressage, cross-country competition, and stadium jumping) is the Holsteiner, a type of German coach horse. Mr. Philip B. Hofmann, having watched with interest the success of these horses in the European shows, decided to import several of the breed, cross them with the Thoroughbred and so produce horses that should do well both in the show ring and in the hunt field.

34. The imported Holstein stallion **Herkules** ridden by Miss Judy Hofmann (later Mrs. Max E. Richter) in the cross-country phase of the Three-Day Event competition at Myopia, in which he placed second. Miss Hofmann kept Herkules for a year at Smith College and trained him both in dressage and jumping. He was always easily handled and gave no trouble when ridden in company with both mares and geldings.

Courtesy of Mr. Philip B. Hofmann

35. Four Hostein horses that are one quarter Thoroughbred, Mr. Hofmann on the box.

Courtesy of Mr. Philip B. Hofmann

Pinto Hunters

Pintos, sometimes known as piebalds (black and white), skewballs (white and any color other than black), paints or colored horses, qualify for registration by their color alone. Since this opens the registration to horses of many breeds, it is not surprising to find outstanding hunters and jumpers as well as three-day horses that are registered in the Pinto book or can obviously qualify for registry. Since many judges prefer Thoroughbreds or Half-breds in the show ring, owners of pintos sometimes find it hard going in hunter classes, but an honest and intelligent judge pins on performance manners, soundness and way of going. (There is no such problem in open jumper classes, of course.) The most famous Pinto in literature is The Pie of National Velvet fame.

36. **Little Miss,** an unregistered Pinto mare, 15:2 hands high, ancestry unknown. This mare was over twenty-six when this picture was taken showing her competing in the Amateur-Owner Hunter class at the Fort Meade Hunt Club Show in 1970, Sherry Canterbury up.

Little Miss, also known as Ladybug, has a most interesting history. She was bought in 1963 by Mrs. Canterbury's mother at the New Holland Auction Sales in Pennsylvania. Because of her age, condition and the fact that her belly was a mass of open sores, plus a very bad disposition which made it dangerous to handle her, she was looked on as suitable only for the killer. So nervous was she that it became necessary to buy a small pony to accompany her home in the van, as she became hysterical.

On arrival, everyone was extremely cautious in handling her. Then one man took a liking to her, slipped on a halter and rode her bareback over a few low jumps. She seemed to take a fancy to jumping and to have great ability, so Mrs. Canterbury decided that even though she had been Western-trained she would turn her into an open jumper. She was shown six months later in open and junior jumping classes and never made a mistake if she could help it.

In 1966 she was Junior Jumper Champion in Maryland. She was very popular with the audience and had many fans because of her peculiar style. While going around the course she would surprise her rider with a series of tremendous bucks, her hind feet going so high that she looked as though she were executing a handstand; then she would chop down on the last three strides before the obstacle, come to almost a dead stop and jump off her hocks. It always looked as though she were quitting, but she cleared the high fences easily. Naturally the crowd loved her, and the more they laughed at her bucking and cheered her jumping the better she liked it.

In 1969, when Little Miss was twenty-five, Mrs. Canterbury deemed it wise to ease off on her open jumping. The little mare loved the show ring so much, however, that her owner decided to try and make her over into a hunter, a seemingly impossible task when one realizes that the most important factors in a hunter are manners and way of going! Surprisingly enough, Ladybug, perhaps to disprove once and for all that old adage about teaching an old dog new tricks, settled down very nicely and soon learned to hack calmly, to omit the fireworks, to maintain an even pace and to stand back and take her fences in her stride. She was particularly successful in the Handy Hunter classes, her early Western training having taught her to stop and turn on a dime and her later open jumping training having taught her to jump from any angle. Even in competition against Thoroughbreds she never failed to be pinned, and at twenty-six she won two reserve championships and fourteen ribbons at the four shows she went to!

Courtesy of Mrs. Sherry Canterbury *Photo by Wilson Holder*

37. **Harlequin,** P-4067, a registered Pinto hunter–jumper, is owned and shown by Miss Naida Whittaker of Seattle. Not only has Harlequin done extremely well in both these divisions, he has also been trained to the fourth level in dressage.

Courtesy of Miss Naida Whittaker

Appaloosa Hunters

The Appaloosa is another of the breeds whose registry is decided on color and markings. These animals were highly prized by the Nez Percé Indians of central Idaho and eastern Washington, who contended that the horn of their hoofs was unusually tough and the animal extremely sturdy. There are several different accepted markings for the Appaloosa. Sometimes they are a mottled grayish brown; more generally they have black or brown spots on a white background. One of the favorite types is the "blanket" marking, which is characterized by a mottled or more or less solid-colored forehand coupled with white quarters strongly marked with the characteristic spots. The skin of the horse is pink, and there is often a pinkish rim of bare skin around the eyes. The hoofs are dark, sometimes with vertical stripes, a marking characteristic of certain of the very early horses. The dark spots can be felt with the fingertips and have given the name of "Raindrop Horse" to the breed. Pictures of what we now call Appaloosas appear in many early paintings, including those of the Lipizzaners. There is no doubt that they originated in the Middle or Far East and were one of the strains brought into Spain by the Moors. Since the original horses to be brought to the New World came from Spain, it is not surprizing to find Appaloosas roaming as wild horses in the western United States in the fifteenth and sixteenth centuries.

38. **Javelin,** #62000551, is a registered Appaloosa sired by High Thunderbird out of Jimmie's Black Feather. Javelin is an excellent type of horse for hunting in almost any country where a rugged, sensible mount is needed. He is shown here being put over the "coffin jump" in the Stadium jumping phase of the New York–Upper Connecticut Regional Rally of the United States Pony Clubs, held in Rhineback, New York. He was purchased from Crestwell Farms, an Appaloosa breeding farm in Virginia, and is being shown by his young owner, Dianne Weber.

Courtesy of Miss Dianne Weber

Pony Hunters

In England, the cradle of hunting, hunting ponies are highly appreciated. Since most of the recognized pony breeds originated in Wales or on the British moors it is not surprising that ever since hunting became a popular sport (not limited to royalty) ponies have had their place. For many years in the United States Shetlands were practically the only breed of pony imported and sold as a suitable children's mount. These ponies, derived from those used to pull coal carts in the mines, were small, thick-necked and, since they were rarely properly trained, being too small for the average adult to ride, soon got the reputation of being extremely stubborn and tricky. Actually they were smart, smart enough to find out very quickly that they were far stronger then the inexperienced children who were expected to manage them.

By selective breeding and the judicious introduction of Welsh, Arabian or Hackney blood, a different type of Shetland pony evolved in the United States. These were known as "American Shetlands." They were much more lightly built than the English variety, being without the broad backs and thick necks. Excellent riding mounts for young riders, they were agile and could scramble whatever they couldn't clear in the hunt field. Of late years breeders, through the introduction of Hackney blood, have reduced the riding Shetland to a miniature high-stepping fine-harness animal, and as such they are shown exclusively by adults, being too high-spirited for a child. There are still good, useful hunting ponies with a certain amount of Shetland in them to be found, but they are usually crossbreds. One often sees such mounts in the Pet Pony division of the shows but only occasionally in the Pony Hunter divisions, which have been taken over almost entirely by the Welsh and Welsh crossbred animals.

The Welsh pony has always been one of the favorite

children's mounts for hunting in England and deservedly so. This pony, which has a good deal of Arabian in his ancestry, is finely built yet sturdy, sensitive without being hysterically so, and very dependable both over fences and on the flat. There are many breeders of Welsh ponies derived from imported stock, and most of these also breed crossbred ponies, either Welsh-Arabian or Welsh-Thoroughbred. These ponies are carefully trained and generally have impeccable dispositions, the kind of animal that will let his young owner climb all over him and play with him as a pet, then go into the show ring or off to a hunt with all the spirit and style of his Arabian ancestors.

Another popular breed of hunting pony, especially in Ireland, is the Connemara pony. He is rugged, sensible and has an enormous jump in him. Exmoor and Dartmoor ponies are also greatly prized, though there are fewer breeders of the Moor ponies in this country than of the Welsh.

The Welsh Pony

39. This registered Welsh mare, **Fairytale,** was bred by Mrs. J. Austin du Pont at Liseter Hall Farm. She was subsequently bought by Mrs. George Oliver of North Kingston, Rhode Island, where she is one of Mrs. Oliver's most reliable school ponies as well as being an outstanding brood mare. She has produced a variety of prize-winning colts and fillies. She is shown here with **Pojac Elf,** who won a first at the Devon (Pennsylvania) Horse Show in the Colt Foal class. Other pictures of Fairytale (Fig. 76) and Elf (Fig. 118) appear in this book.

Courtesy of Mrs. George T. Oliver *Photo by Tarrance*

40. This beautiful Welsh head, reflecting the Arabian ancestry which is introduced from time to time to refine the native ponies, belongs to **Pojac Merlyn Myth,** one of Mrs. Oliver's registered Welsh ponies, shown with Jennifer Curry.

Courtesy of Mrs. George T. Oliver *Photo by Colin H. Brearley*

41. **Cusop Sheriff,** B-11466, is one of the most sought-after Welsh stallions. By Cusop Call Boy out of Coed Coch Brenhines Sheba, he is owned by Mrs. Karl D. Butler of Ithaca, New York. He was first in Section B for Welsh stallions at the National Welsh Show in 1964 and was Reserve Champion in the same show in 1970.

Courtesy of Mrs. Karl D. Butler

42. Cusop Sheriff under tack. Notice his alert yet quiet way of going. This stallion has produced prize-winning hunter ponies all over North America, from California to Rhode Island and from Canada to Alabama. They all inherit his beautiful disposition, making sensible ponies with good conformation and plenty of substance. His rider is Linda Sue Butler.

Courtesy of Mrs. Karl D. Butler

43. **GlanNant Saga,** B-13974, 13:2 hands. This is a beautiful Welsh pony hunter mare, B Division, by Cusop Sheriff out of Coed Coch Prydyddes. This mare has done exceptionally well in Pony Hunter classes. She is a good example of the result of breeding Cusop Sheriff to a large pony mare, ensuring a foal which will be eligible for the B Division of Welsh pony classes. Large ponies to show in this division must measure not less than 13:3 hands or over 14:1.

Courtesy of Mrs. Karl D. Butler

44. **Findeln Miss Muffet,** B-15339, by Brockwell Spider out of Catherston Blue Gown, with foal **GlanNant Curdo,** B-21425, by Cusop Sheriff, shown winning the large Pony Hunter Brood Mare Championship at the Canadian Breeders' show at King, Ontario, in 1970. She is owned by GlanNant Farm.

Courtesy of Mrs. Karl D. Butler *Photo by William Kinson*

45. **Liseter Bright Flash,** #3451, shown at the 1968 Devon (Pennsylvania) Horse Show, exhibits perfect Welsh conformation. He was foaled in 1958 and is by Liseter Bright Light out of the imported mare Coed Coch Sigldin. He was Supreme Champion at the Royal Winter Fair in Toronto, Ontario, Canada, in 1967 and has also won one Champion of All Breeds and seven Grand Champions, as well as a number of reserves, twenty-one firsts, and sixteen seconds. He was bred and is owned by the Liseter Hall Farm, one of the outstanding Welsh breeding farms in the United States, the project of Mrs. J. Austin du Pont of Newtown Square, Pennsylvania. Mrs. du Pont breeds both purebred Welsh and crossbreds (Welsh–Thoroughbreds).

Courtesy of Liseter Hall Farm *Photo by Budd*

46. **Liseter Flyndwr Fay,** #1873, winning the Brood Mare Championship at Devon in 1970, is another of Mrs. du Pont's outstanding Welsh ponies that has produced many winners.

Courtesy of Liseter Hall Farm *Photo by Freudy*

47. Mrs. du Pont driving her magnificent Welsh four-in-hand. The leaders are Liseter Bright Crocus and Liseter Star Flower; the wheelers are Liseter Star Fashion and Liseter Twinkle. All these ponies follow the hounds as well as compete in Hunter Pony and Welsh Pony classes in the United States and in Canada.

Courtesy of Liseter Hall Farm *Photo by Freudy*

48. Three generations of du Ponts in a family class with Mrs. J. Austin du Pont in command. All those in the picture hunt and/or show.

Courtesy of Liseter Hall Farm *Photo by Tarrance*

The Connemara Pony

The Irish Connemara Pony has been famed as a hunter in his native land, the Galway section of Ireland, for many years. The most famous ever imported was Little Squire, a 13-hand animal (some say smaller) that beat the top open jumpers in the United States and Canada during the thirties and early forties. He was a very hot little pony, and it was astounding to watch him come into a jump that looked considerably taller than he did and with fiery nostrils soar over it.

49. This Connemara mare, **Shadow Gray,** with Shelley Emery up, is shown winning the Reserve Championship, Large Hunter Pony Division, at the 1967 Erie, Pennsylvania, Show.

Courtesy of Mrs. John Emery

The American Shetland Pony

50. **Belle Meade Ultima Thule,** an American Shetland bred at the Belle Meade Farm in Virginia, is really not typical of the American Shetlands for which that farm was noted in the 1920s and 1930s. However, he was such a charming pony and so reliable that I have included his picture. He was never shown (in those days there were no classes for ponies in New England) and doubtless would never have been successful, but he was one of the favorite ponies on our place and was called Dandy Beans for that reason. He is pictured here with Shirley Self (later Mrs. John O. Brotherhood, Jr.), Huntsman for the Point O'Forks Farm Bloodhounds.

Photo by Sydney B. Self, Jr.

51. **Belle Meade Success** is a much more typical example of the old-style American Shetland. Forty-two inches high, Shoebutton, as he was called, could get over the rough Connecticut country as easily as the tallest Thoroughbred. Whatever he couldn't fly he scrambled or ducked under. He treated the rough stone walls as the Irish hunters do, changing legs on the top. He and his young ride, Toby Self, played the part of Mr. Fox in the Fox Movietone Short Short which has been shown all over the world. The little stallion was the constant companion of his young master, who inherited him from his older brother. He lived to be thirty years old and was sound in wind and limb until the sad day when he had to be put down because his back teeth had worn away and he could no longer masticate. Had there been a local horse dentist to fit him with a bridge (as has been done before), he might be living yet. On the ground behind Shoey's back feet lies Rip the bloodhound (see Fig. 11).

Half-Bred and Crossbred Hunters

As explained, many countries are too rough for hunting the average Thoroughbred. Also an admixture of Thoroughbred with some other bloodlines usually produces a wiser, sounder and more sensible animal. The following pictures are of horses of mixed breeding that have all proved themselves as hunters.

52. The leading horse in this very beautiful photograph of the Moore County Hounds leaving kennels is **Battlewick,** whose photo has appeared earlier (Fig. 18) and will appear again. He was foaled at the Remount Station in Virginia, his sire being the Thoroughbred Battleship, owned by Mrs. Marion du Pont Scott, who donated one service to the top remount mare of that year. This mare, Battlewick's dam, was Hotwick out of Campfire. As a young stallion Batllewick was sent to run with the army range horses in New Mexico. Then, when the remount program was discontinued, he was bought by Cappy Smith, the famous rider and trainer, and was shown by him and by Alex Calvert as an open jumper. Mile-Away Farms bought him as a nine-year-

old and Mrs. Moss hunted him through his seventeenth year. She showed him in hunter trials before stallions were prohibited in the hunter divisions of recognized shows. At the Moore County Hunter Trials he was reserve to Gift of Gold, the Steeplechase Horse of the Year. His history as sire of outstanding stakes winners and champions in the horse show world is phenomenal, and at the age of 25 he was still in great demand. In 1971 these included Manley, stakes winner, and Royal Citation, top three-year-old in the shows, others in the same category being Sandhill Flight, Flying Liberty, Liberty Award and Long Leaf, all top winners in 1970.

Photo by Emerson Humphrey

53. **Jester,** shown crossing a stream under the capable hands of Miss Lili Francklyn, is a fifteen-year-old Thoroughbred–Quarter Horse cross. He has hunted eight years with the Litchfield County Hounds in Connecticut, where the going is very trappy. This photo was taken at the Glastonbury Pony Club Combined Training Event. The year before, Jester was high-scoring C horse at the Regional Rally at Old Chatham, New York.

Thoroughbred on Quarter Horse is often a most successful cross, producing excellent hunters and jumpers. The less desirable qualities of the colder-blooded Quarter Horse are refined, the staying power of the Thoroughbred is retained, while the latter's oversensitivity, both physical and temperamental, is reduced bythe Quarter Horse blood. The agility of the Quarter Horse also is valuable in a country where the going is heavy and the rider in the hunt field may find himself in the type of sticky situation that might endanger a horse of pure Thoroughbred breeding.

Courtesy of Mrs. Reginal Francklyn *Photo by Duffy*

54. **Snaps of Gold,** by the Thoroughbred Wrack of Gold out of Lady Rocket (the latter by a Thoroughbred stallion out of an American Saddle mare of the Flash Peavine strain), is thus a three quarter-bred. He got his name because he snapped at his owner, Mrs. Oliver, when he was less than a minute old, nor has he lost this habit with his years. He has won many hunter and jumper ribbons in Rhode Island, as well as fifty championships and thirty-six reserve championships. Other details of Snaps's career are given under Figures 78 and 87–89.

Courtesy of Mrs. George T. Oliver *Photo by Duffy*

55. **Wickeri,** A-49786, half-Arabian registry, sire Aazrak, Arabian registry, dam, Lassy, crossbred, with Miss Robin Stemler up. Wickeri was a five-year-old in 1970. She was bought by Miss Stemler as a three-year-old and shown successfully both in recognized and unrecognized shows. In the latter as a three-year-old her first season she was champion and reserve many times against all sorts of competition. She has also won in hunter trials and is a splendid example of an Arabian crossbred hunter type.

Courtesy of Miss Robin Stemler *Photo by John E. Zimmerman*

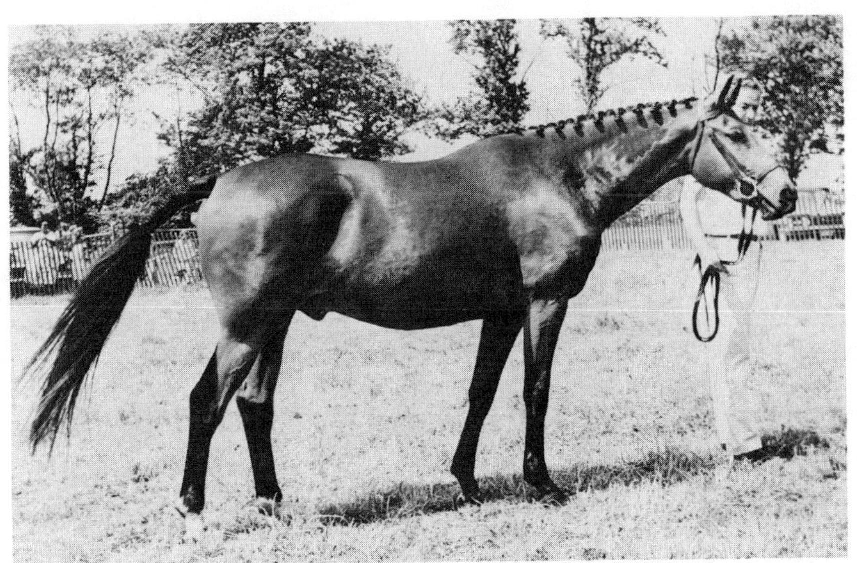

56. **Hyllis,** by the Holstein stallion Herkules out of the Thoroughbred mare Kay-O-Mine, as a two-year-old. This particular cross is not common in the United States, and it will be interesting to see what success these horses have in the show rings and hunt fields in the next few years. Mr. Hofmann, who became interested in the breed and imported the sire of Hyllis, feels that they have a great future.

Courtesy of Mr. Philip B. Hofmann *Photo by Carl Klein*

57. Hyllis, shown as a Hunter in the Branchville Show, presents a pleasing picture as she clears the obstacle calmly, smoothly and with little effort. She is being ridden by Mrs. Max Richter, formerly Miss Judy Hofmann.

Courtesy of Mr. Philip B. Hofmann *Photo by Budd*

The Canadian country offers a challenge. It is not the open, galloping country that we find in the South or in England but more nearly resembles some of the country of New England (especially Connecticut) and New York. There is a lot of woodland, the fields are not large, and sometimes the going is both rocky and muddy. Most of the fences are paneled with some form of wooden obstacle—sawn logs upended, for example, or even roots of trees. In this it reflects the big timber industry. Because of the necessity of paneling, riders must wait their turns at the jumps, something which is hard for a nervous Thoroughbred to put up with, especially on a cold and frosty morning. Nor is the Thoroughbred well adapted physically to the country; his tendons are too fragile. So most working hunters in Canada have at least some cold (draft) blood in their veins. They are steady, intelligent, extremely sturdy and yet they have plenty of ambition and, though not always very fast, are well up to staying with hounds across the short fields and winding trails. Of course, for show purposes there are many purebred Canadian hunters, some of which do hunt, but the rider must be ever aware of their weaknesses. As a rule he cannot relax and listen to the music of the hounds, depending on the good will, stamina and intelligence of his horse to carry him through the day's hunting.

58. **Cossack,** a Canadian-bred mare by a Thoroughbred sire out of a draft dam, was bred and trained near Ottawa and later went to Toronto, where she was successfully hunted by members of the hunt staff for many years. Col. McKibbon is up.

Courtesy of Col. and Mrs. Arthur McKibbon

59. Here we see Col. McKibbon, MFH of the Frontenac Hunt at Kingston, Ontario, Canada, on **Mohawk,** another Canadian Half-bred.

Courtesy of Col. and Mrs. Arthur McKibbon

60. Canadian Half-breds are noted not only for their stamina, substance and staying power but for their longevity. This is Sundance, by a Thoroughbred out of a Belgian mare. He was hunted for four years with the Ottawa Hunt and then with the Frontenac Hunt. He is shown here at the age of twenty-five, Mrs. McKibbon, Whipper-in, up.

Courtesy of Col. and Mrs. Arthur McKibbon

61. There is no more sagacious, honest and safe hunter in the world than the Irish hireling. Beautiful he may not be, but he will take care both of himself and of his rider in what sometimes seems to be a completely impossible situation. This picture shows the author on one of the many hirelings she rode during several hunting holidays in southern Ireland in the 1950s. Most of these animals are farm bred but virtually all have some Thoroughbred blood in their veins, for it is the custom of the owners of stud farms to give local farmers free service from their choice stallions. This ensures a plentitude of available hunters to the "gentry" and their guests, as well as to local lads, when the hunting season rolls around. Virtually every male in Ireland is inter-

ested in fox or stag hunting. Farmers who formerly found a market for their half-breds by selling them to the army have no trouble now in renting them to visitors who come to acquaint themselves with a type of hunting that cannot be bettered or, in the mind of this writer, equaled in any other part of the world. For the most part such visitors arrive at the meet to be awaited by an animal such as the one shown here that they have never seen before and knowing that they will be confronted by types of obstacles that they have never encountered in the United States. They need have no fears. These plain-looking hirelings will scramble out of a bog that reaches to their bellies and up the side of a steep bank with never a bit of solid ground to give firm footing; they will change legs on top of a County Limerick stone wall, landing amid a mass of fallen and falling rock without touching one, push through the hairiest bank and clear a drain ten feet deep and as wide from a standstill! If bred and hunted in the Galway country they will fly the high, lacelike stone walls unperturbed by an unexpected drop of eight or ten feet on the far side. Nor does water frighten them, for I have seen them plunge into a river, disappear completely from sight and come up just as ready to tackle the next!

62. **Blackacre Christopher,** a fine example of a crossbred hunter pony suitable both for showing and hunting. His sire is Devan Marsh Hawk, the registered Morgan pictured in Figure 28, and his dam is Blackacre's Deborah, a half-Arabian mare. He is shown here in a pair class at the Bath Horse Show at Bob-O-Lin Farm in Bath, Ohio, with David Pittenger up.

Courtesy of Blackacre Farm *Photo by Leslie Howard*

Part III

Training

63. Fortunate is the foal whose future career lies in the hunt field or in the hunter division of show competition. For him there will be no set tails, no nail-studded boots, no forcing of his jumping ability to the point where the impossible is demanded of him. Nor will he be galloped under saddle when his bones are still soft and his tendons prone to injury. He will be handled from birth in such a fashion that he will never fear man but learn to trust him in emergencies. His early days, like those of other foals, will be spent beside his mother. But his pasture will be the wide, sunny fields of the stud farm covered with the richest and most nutritious grass, chosen especially to develop strong bones and healthy bodies. His only frustration will be that his fuzzy tail is not always long enough to reach and dislodge the annoying flies.

When the summer sun beats down too strongly, he will make his way through shady paths with his playfellows, . . .

. . . to cool his feet in a swiftly flowing stream.

Courtesy of Mr. R. C. Winmill *Photos by Anthony Lanza*

64. When foalhood is over he will continue to play in the pastures until his bones are hardened and will stand the training that lies before him. Thoroughbreds destined for flat racing are broken to the saddle as yearlings and raced as two-year-olds. The result is that most racehorses are ready for retirement at seven or eight, many break down long before that, and it is rare to see a horse, raced as a two-year-old, that does not develop bowed tendons, thoroughpins or other ailments at an age when the young hunter is just coming into the most useful years of his life. Consequently, instead of being retired as seven- or eight-year-olds, many hunters are to be seen still soaring over obstacles in the show ring or following a fast-moving pack from covert to covert several times a week at the age of twenty or so.

These animals are allowed to mature at least until the age of three before any serious work is required of them, and many trainers prefer to wait until their young stock is four or even five before they allow them to do anything other than work on the flat under light weight, free jump without a rider in a Hitchcock pen or hop over a very low obstacle now and again under a light rider.

The colts shown in pasture are the produce of the Blackacre Farm in Ohio, where Mr. and Mrs. T. E. Pittenger breed and raise Thoroughbreds and Morgans for hunting, showing, pleasure and occasionally for racing as well. The one on the far left is a yearling by a Thoroughbred stallion out of an American Saddle Horse mare. He was later trained as an Event horse and is now owned by William Lorimer of Cleveland, Ohio. The colt on the right, Forgery, is a Thoroughbred by This Evening out of Beverly Blue and is owned by Lee Thibodeau of Presque Isle, Maine. Event horses are trained for cross-country work over natural fences, stadium jumping and dressage. They compete in what are known as Three Phase Event or Combined Training competitions. This type of class is one of the events in the Olympic Games and other international competitions.

Courtesy of Blackacre Farm

65. A hunter has much to learn besides how to jump. Early in life he is introduced to his future hunting companions, the hounds. Long before his blood is stirred by the sound of the huntsman's horn and the music of the pack in full cry, he is ridden on paths and trails with a hound at heel. Thus does he learn never to commit that most heinous crime of all, one which will bring the well-deserved wrath of any Master—namely, the injury of a hound by the misbehavior of an ill-trained or awkward horse.

This is Devan Marsh Hawk, the Morgan stallion owned by the Blackacre Farm, accompanied by his favorite hound, Young Ruben. Miss Nancy Pittenger is up. Though the stallion has long since learned his manners, he and his rider often take to the quiet trails when the hunting season is over. Hawk is not only a prize-winning hunter himself but is the progenitor of many other fine working hunters. He also appears in Figures 28, 73 and 91.

Courtesy of Blackacre Farm *Photo by Robert A. Boyajian*

66. A few Thoroughbreds, after a brief preparation for racing, with possibly a little experience on the track, are found to be unsuitable for that career. If the decision is made before their delicate legs have been injured, they are often sold to those interested in training them as field hunters or for showing. Such a one is Harvest Lassie, shown here with Mrs. Trudi Janney up. This filly is having her first cross-country gallop on a brisk fall day with a premature blizzard arriving to add to her excitement.

Courtesy of St. Finnbarr Farm

67. Next comes Harvest Lassie's introduction to water as, with much splashing, she crosses a narrow stream.

Courtesy of St. Finnbarr Farm

68. Several weeks later, her excitement and fears lulled, we see her wading placidly downstream in water breast deep. St. Finnbarr Farm is in Colorado. Horses of many different breeding backgrounds are to be found there undergoing training for hunting, jumping and showing. It is also an equitation center, and the animals are used for that purpose as well. As some of their stock is Western trained and bought after maturity, the Janneys face the double problem of building confidence in human beings in animals which may not have been handled until the age of two or more, and of teaching a Western-trained horse, taught to work on a slack rein, to accept the bit and listen to the signals of the rider transmitted through it. Thus lessons which should have been learned long ago must now be introduced before the prospective hunter learns to be quiet, well-mannered and unafraid in all circumstances.

Courtesy of St. Finnbarr Farm

69. In Rhode Island Mrs. Oliver, who uses Thoroughbreds, registered Welsh ponies, Welsh–Arabians and Welsh–Thoroughbreds in her school, also believes in a lot of cross-country work for her young riders and their mounts to teach boldness and to steady them.

Like the St. Finnbarr horses, these ponies are also taught not to be afraid of water, and after the cross-country ride the young equestriennes wade their mounts into the water of the wide river that laps the shoreline.

Courtesy of Mrs. George T. Oliver

70. Work over cavaletti develops balance, rhythm and impulsion. It regulates the stride and calms the horse that tends to get excited when first presented with a bar that must be crossed. This is Nancy Pittenger again, on Debt. Nancy balances in the stirrups to free the horse's haunches and encourage her to keep her balance forward and her head low. Debt, working barefoot, shows good knee and hock action and is obviously alert without being nervous.

Courtesy of Blackacre Farm *Photo by Robert A. Boyajian*

71. Lissa, a Welsh-Arabian crossbred, trots over slightly higher cavaletti. Notice the construction of the obstacles. Simply by rotating them the bars can be raised from six to eighteen inches.

Courtesy of Mrs. George T. Oliver *Photo by M. C. Self*

72. Longeing plays a large part in the training of the hunter, and even after years of experience it is often advisable to return the animal to the longe. Without a rider the horse jumps freely, using his head, neck and back more flexibly than when handicapped by weight on his back. Here Lissa is first longed past the obstacles a few times, the trainer placing herself so that the longe forms a continuation of the bar of the jump.

When the pupil is calm yet attentive the trainer steps forward a few steps on the approach, thus putting the horse in line with the obstacle and making it easier for her to jump than to avoid it. Her ears come forward . . .

. . . and she jumps quietly and in stride, undisturbed by the sudden descent of a stirrup which slid down the leather at exactly the wrong moment.

Photos by M. C. Self

73. A trainer of young horses must always be prepared for an unexpectedly long takeoff. Devan Marsh Hawk, the Morgan hunter stallion, has so much jump in him that he occasionally jumps his young rider, J. David Craig, completely out of the saddle! However, the boy is sufficiently experienced to enable him to keep his hands down and not get left behind in such a crisis.

Courtesy of Blackacre Farm *Photo by Robert A. Boyajian*

74. Harvest Lassie of St. Finnbarr Farm, whom we saw earlier working on the flat, is now ready to try a few obstacles set up in the woodsy trails. Since she is still very green, the rider dismounts and leads her up to a low fence. Far from being disturbed by the sight of the obstacle, Lassie seems more interested in something off to her right.

Farther along they come to a low in-and-out which Lassie takes calmly.

Courtesy of St. Finnbarr Farm

75. Another St. Finnbarr prospect is this young Thoroughbred Ratinto. He started his career as a lead pony on the track. In that capacity he led the procession of nervous racehorses from the assembly ring to the starting gate. Now he is receiving training that will make him into a field hunter, a contestant in hunter classes at the shows, or both. The jump is of sawed-up logs, an unusual obstacle except in parts of the West and in Canada.

Courtesy of St. Finnbarr Farm

76. Mrs. Oliver holds Bonanza, a registered Welsh, 11:3 hands in height, so that he and his young rider, Wendy O'Brian, age ten, may judge the height of the low chicken-coop jump. Meanwhile Fairytale, a Welsh mare bred at Liseter Hall Farm, and her rider, Jane Plimpton, take a good look at it on their own.

Knowing what to expect, the children and their ponies fly the little hurdle with perfect confidence.

Photos by M. C. Self

77. Ditches as obstacles are not too common either in New England or in the show ring. But since they do occur occasionally, especially on outside courses and hunter trials, hunters must be trained to take them willingly. Sunny Day, also bred at Liseter Hall Farm and owned by Mrs. Oliver, hesitates for a second on the brink of a newly constructed ditch edged with twelve-by-twelve timber . . .

. . . but her young rider, Ellen Tetlow, boots him on and he flies it. Sunny Day is a Welsh-Thoroughbred cross, 13:2 hands in height.

Now it's the turn of Fancy Pants, a Welsh-Arabian crossbred. He does not hesitate, but his jumping style is somewhat reminiscent of that so often depicted in old English hunting prints. His rider is Pam Turner.

Company builds confidence, and here we see Sunny Day and Fancy Pants over the same obstacle, now jumping in stride without hesitation.

Photos by M. C. Self

78. Learning to jump abreast over such an obstacle as this whose elements are varied in height is particularly valuable training, both for the prospective hunter and for the rider. Since the mounts also vary in size, stride and way of going and since all start on signal abreast, it is up to the riders to so rate them that regardless of whether the natural stride of each individual animal is long or short, the temperament eager or sluggish, each must take his assigned panel exactly at the same instant as his fellows. In the air together from left to right we see Fancy Pants, Lissa, Snaps of Gold and Puck. Snaps of Gold, introduced in Figure 54, is the gelding owned by Mrs. Oliver that has been the winner of many hunter championships. Puck is full brother to Fancy Pants.

After circling the field at the gallop, they take a different and much easier obstacle.

Photos by M. C. Self

79. The well-schooled hunter should be prepared to take any type of obstacle willingly. (April in) Fairbanks, a registered Appaloosa, is shown clearing an old wagon body topped by a bar and with a large galvanized drainpipe under it to add interest. The rider, Jill Williams, who later bought him, is now hunting him regularly with the Roaring Pack Hounds in Colorado.

Courtesy of St. Finnbarr Farm

80. Battlewick, under the capable hands of W. O. Moss, MFH, Moore County Hounds, shows how it should be done. He is the aged Half-bred stallion introduced in Figures 18 and 52. Chicken coops such as this are common obstacles both in the show ring and in the hunting field. However, in the latter they are usually set in a fence and form a panel. Without wings and placed in the open, such as shown here, they are an invitation to a shy-out. One would expect two such veterans as these to take such an obstacle in fine form and without hesitation, and one is not disappointed.

Courtesy of Page Shamburger *Photo by Budd*

81. Battlewick hunted until he was seventeen. Perhaps Detinue, the Morgan filly shown here as a four-year-old, will some day look back on just as illustrious a career. Here Debbie Shepard has brought her to the Erlenhoff Stables fall show. Seen in this background and pose, one can well imagine her standing at a covert side alertly waiting for the ta-ra-ra-ra-ra of the horn and the music of the hounds to signal that the fox has gone away.

Courtesy of Blackacre Farm *Photo by George Shepard*

Part IV

Shows, Trials and Steeplechases

Horse Shows

Statistics show that there are more horses in the United States today than ever before, and this after it was predicted that the advent of the automobile and the tractor meant the knell of the horse. Two sports are responsible: the horse show and the race track. And of the two the former has had the wider effect since breeders of all types and breeds of horses and ponies continue to produce hundreds of thousands of animals for this purpose. Those that do not make winners in the ring are sold as pleasure horses or as hunters.

So popular has the horse show become that, especially in the larger registered affairs, the classes are so big that they present a real problem. Also the competition is such that one must spend a great deal of money, first to buy or breed an animal that can win and second to have him trained by a professional. He may also need to be shown by a professional as well, depending on his breed. These conditions may seriously threaten the recognized horse show scheduling as we know it today. Already we have cumulative point classes such as the Medal and MacClay Horsemanship classes, in which contestants must have won a specified number of blue ribbons at other recognized shows in order to compete at the National Horse Show in Madison Square Garden. Perhaps, in the future, before entering any recognized show, a contestant will have to win or place in an unrecognized show first. Since keeping a horse as a family pet in the back yard has become more and more popular and since few of these are quality show animals, it is only to be expected that this clique of enthusiastic young horsewomen and horsemen will soon begin organizing their own local shows. It seems all to the good that there be more local shows at which young people or others who like to train and show their own horses can compete without coming up against what is virtually professional competition.

82. There is a nice relaxed atmosphere about a country horse show that is most pleasing. Instead of the emphasis being entirely on winning, with the complaints and ill will one sometimes finds at larger shows, there is a feeling of sportsmanship and goodwill. The show depicted is being held on the grounds of the Horse and Buggy Club in Holliston, Massachusetts, and two classes are being judged simultaneously. In the middle foreground is a Western Pair class; beyond, a Hunter class is being judged on conformation and soundness. The rings are formed with snow fence, which can be

easily removed and put up in another part of the grounds or simply stored until needed again. Note that the outside course for hunters includes jumps inside the rings as well as obstacles set in the outside fences. Beyond these two brush jumps, a gate and a concrete wall with a striped pole rider. No doubt contestants are required to enter over the far hedge, circle within the outer fences of the two rings, jumping the other brush and the gate, then, after leaving over the striped pole, continue on more jumps in the field. The spectators and their cars are safely ensconced on the little knoll in the background, from which they have a good view of both arenas. The horse vans are accommodated in another section on the right. Contestants waiting to enter can warm up outside the rings as Mrs. Oliver, riding Snaps of Gold, is shown doing here. At the same time they can also keep an eye on how the show is progressing.

Courtesy of Mrs. George T. Oliver *Photo by Joseph P. Vrabel*

83. **Sign The Card,** a bay mare, 15:3 hands, six years old in 1971, is one of the outstanding show hunters of today. In 1969 she won the American Horse Shows Association high score awards in Green Working Hunter Championship with 1,297 points, a record, and Amateur-Owner Championship with 1,568 points, also a record. That year she had 58 champion and reserve ribbons with 128 blue ribbons. She was Champion at Madison Square Garden and Grand Champion at the Washington International Show. In 1970 she continued her outstanding performance in the ring, winning the AHSA Amateur-Owner Championship again with 1,926 points, a new record, and second-year Green Working Hunter Championship. She was Grand Champion Green Working Hunter as well as Grand Champion Hunter with 2,454 points, an all-time record. The Virginia Horse Shows Association awarded her their Green Hunter Championship and Amateur-Owner Championship, she was Grand Champion for the second time at the Washington International Show, and in two years she collected a total of 104 championships and reserves, 9 high score championships and 246 blues. This mare is by Double Hitch out of Princess Ala. Her owner-rider is Miss Jane E. Womble and her trainer is Walter J. Lee of Belcort Farm, Keswick, Virginia.

Courtesy of Miss Womble and the American Horse Shows Association

84. **Moonlight Murmur,** a lovely gray mare, is by the English stallion Blue Murmur out of the Canadian mare Silvos. She was foaled in 1960 and is seven-eighths Thoroughbred, being a fourth cross of Thoroughbred and German coachhorse. Her stable name is Granny, and she is owned by Mrs. Ivor Stoddard of No View Farm, Aiken, South Carolina.

Mrs. Stoddard writes that Moonlight Murmur was purchased as a three-year-old by John Hosang of Aiken and sold to Miss Sally Tucker, who sold her to Mrs. Stoddard's mother for Mrs. Stoddard, who was Miss Linda Brandt before her marriage, the mare being, at this time, in the hands of Bucky Reynolds for training. Mr. Reynolds continued as trainer and Miss Brandt showed her from July, 1964, to July, 1966, under her maiden name. After her marriage to Mr. Stoddard to No View Stables, (later No View Farm), she was shown under the No View name. In 1964 and 1966 Miss Brandt showed her extensively in such far-separated shows as Detroit, Hot Springs, Lake City (Florida), Gross Pointe, Warrenton, Richmond, and North Shore. She won many championships and reserves at these places, never being out of the ribbons. In 1966 she showed only eleven times, winning six championships and five reserves. In 1967 she was

85. **Magic Parade** is a chestnut gelding, 16:2 hands, foaled in 1965. This typy young hunter is by Parade out of Near Magic. His owner is Mrs. George Sloan of Brentwood, Tennessee, his trainer Walter J. Lee. We see him here being ridden by Miss Jane E. Womble. Magic Parade was shown as a first-year green hunter in 1970, when he won the American Horse Shows Association championship in that division. He collected fifty-four ribbons in all, including twenty championships and reserves. With such an outstanding beginning there is no doubt that Magic Parade has a fine future before him.

Courtesy of Miss Womble and the American Horse Shows Association

---

shown in only six shows but nevertheless placed fourth in the AHSA Amateur standings. She took third place in the Virginia standings, though she showed in only two shows in that state that year. As of February, 1971, Granny has been retired from the show ring and is expected to make an equally glorious name for herself as a brood mare on the Stoddards' stud farm.

Courtesy of Mr. and Mrs. Ivor Stoddard *Photo by Budd*

86. Another outstanding young working hunter from Belcort Farm is **Perfect Stranger,** also owned and ridden by Miss Womble and trained by Walter Lee. He won the 1968 Virginia Horse Shows Association Green Working Hunter Championship and the Junior Hunter Reserve Championship. In 1969 he was the VHSA Small Hunter Hunter Champion and was the Green Working Hunter Grand Champion at the Washington International Show. In 1970 he was Champion Amateur-Owner at Madison Square Garden. Perfect Stranger is a gray gelding, 15:2 hands, foaled in 1965.

Courtesy of Miss Jan E. Womble *Photo by Budd*

87. **Snaps of Gold,** owned by Mrs. George T. Oliver and trained from birth by her, was foaled in 1957. Mrs. Oliver started showing Snaps seriously in 1962, and by 1964 he had won 300 blue ribbons, 115 reds and 161 of lower denominations, most being acquired in Rhode Island shows. He has retired two challenge trophies, the Sciarrotta Working Hunter Trophy and the Doris R. Schlink Trail Horse Trophy. He has won fifty championships and thirty-six reserve championships, ten Rhode Island high score awards and five Rhode Island reserve high score awards. Some of these championships and reserves have been in the Working Hunter division, others in Pleasure and Trail Horse. Shown by Mary Grosvenor, a pupil of Mrs. Oliver, Snaps has been equally successful in the junior divisions, both in Hack and Working Hunter classes. We see him here at the Horse and Buggy Show.

Mrs. Oliver runs a riding school in North Kingston, Rhode Island, and Snaps is very much of a member of it. He also appears in Figures 54, 78 and 82.

Courtesy of Mrs. George T. Oliver *Photo by Ken Ross, Sr.*

88. At fourteen years and with eleven seasons of showing behind him Snaps of Gold ends the 1971 season with three more Rhode Island championships: Junior Working Hunter, Trail Horse and the Overall Rhode Island Championship. "It is time for us both to retire," says Mrs. Oliver.

Courtesy of Mrs. George T. Oliver *Photo by Colin H. Brearley*

89. But one wonders about next year and the year after too when one sees the joyful expression on the face of both owner and mount at being awarded yet another blue. After all, we have pictured several horses that are well into their twenties and still showing.

Courtesy of Mrs. George T. Oliver *Photo by Duffy*

90. **Li-Ke,** by Battlewick out of Honolulu Moon, was bred by John Kibbler of Raleigh, North Carolina, who sold him as a two-year-old to J. Arthur Reynolds of Warrenton, Virginia. Mr. Reynolds's daughter, Betty Oare, showed him in Green Conformation Hunter classes in 1967 and 1968 and won consistently with him. In July in the latter year he was purchased by Miss Cornelia Guest of New Canaan, Connecticut. She showed him in 1969 in the Junior Hunter division, and her instructress, Patricia Heuckeroth, showed him in the Regular Hunter division of that year. Miss Heuckeroth continued showing in the latter division in 1970, and not only did Li-Ke win Champion or Reserve in fifteen out of twenty shows, his rider was declared AHSA "Horsewoman of the Year."

Among his many outstanding performances Li-Ke won every jumping class in his division at Upperville, Virginia, and was champion at such far-separated shows as Atlanta, Georgia; Ox Ridge, Connecticut; Sussex County, New Jersey, as well as at the Toronto, Canada, Royal Winter Fair. He was High Score Champion and Regular Working Hunter Champion

91. Mrs. T. E. Pittenger of Blackacre Farm takes her prize-winning Morgan stallion Devan Marsh Hawk for a promenade around the show grounds. Though all Morgans are not trained as Hunters and not many that are do as well in the shows as Hawk, he is proof that certain of the blood can succeed in the Hunter division.

Courtesy of Blackacre Farm

---

of the American Horse Shows Association and also Virginia Horse Shows Association regular Working Hunter Champion. Li-Ke's sire, Battle Wick, appears several times in this book, and this picture of a so-successful son proves the prepotence of his illustrious sire.

Courtesy of Miss Cornelia Guest *Photo by Budd*

92. **The Cub** is a 15:2-hand Half-bred. He was first schooled as an open jumper and is shown here competing at the Boulder Brook, N.J., Fall Show in the early 1940s with his owner, George M. Hudson, up. However, though he was consistently in the jump-offs, he could not be counted on to clear five and a half feet every time. He was retired as an open horse and next made his debut as a hunter, where he was eminently successful. He finally wound up his varied career as lead pony to the well-known Count Fleet.

Courtesy of Mr. Hudson and the Pinto Horse Association
Photo by Ira Haas

93. **Harlequin,** an outstanding Tobiano Pinto, was hunted regularly and shown both as a hunter and a jumper with great success in the 1960s. His rider is Bobby Burke and he is owned by Mrs. Winston Guest.

Courtesy of Mrs. Guest and the Pinto Horse Association
Photo by Allen—Middleburg, Va.

94. **Checkmate,** a registered Pinto mare, P-13659, is here shown as a hunter by her owner, Miss Irene Hurlbert. This is one of the "English" Pintos, as opposed to the squarer, Western type usually having more Quarter Horse ancestry. Checkmate looks as though she had American Saddle and possibly some Arabian blood. Although this books deals only with the horse, I cannot resist commenting also on the beautiful position of the rider.

Courtesy of Miss Hurlbert and the Pinto Horse Association
Photo by Gail E. Bliss

95. Another example of a horse that started in the racing game and changed to the hunt field is this very beautiful conformation hunter. **Boyne Valley,** TB # 636861. Canadian bred, he is by Royal Vale out of Lovely Thoughts, the latter by Mimelech. This photo was taken at the 1969 Oak Brook National Show. He was a six-year-old at the time and is being shown under the capable guidance of Miss Judy Mangin.

Boyne Valley is owned by Mr. and Mrs. J. E. Cottrelle of Toronto, Ontario, Canada. He is 16:3 hands and was bought as a conformation hunter prospect out of steeplechase training for the Cottrelles by Max Bonham. In 1969 he was Green Conformation Hunter Champion in the United States.

Courtesy of Mrs. Max Bonham

96. Ratinto (registered name, Parsons Luck), introduced in Figure 75, is shown here placing in the Coxtail Horse Show in 1970, Open Hunter Division. One year earlier he was ponying racehorses at Ruidoso, New Mexico.

Courtesy of St. Finnbarr Farm *Photo by Dick King*

97. We saw the Thoroughbred filly Blue Hour in Figure 20 as a yearling. Here she is winning the 1969 Long Island Professional Horseman's Association Green Working Hunter Championship (with more than double the points earned by the reserve horse in that division) with Harry de Leyer up. She is owned by Mrs. Nina Brandsema and was purchased from Mr. and Mrs. T. E. Pittenger of Blackacre Farm.

Courtesy of Blackacre Farm

98. Placing in the Fort Leavenworth Show as a Working Hunter is My Duke, ridden by Becky Cenac. The Fort Leavenworth hunter course is well designed: the terrain is uneven, partly wooded and partly in open fields; the obstacles are typical of those normally encountered in actual hunting conditions. Many shows cannot, because of physical limitations, really test the ability of a horse to work over hilly terrain and such courses are usually reserved for hunter trials.

Photo by Guy Kassal

99. Mr. Jack Frey on Rafter D. San negotiates a different obstacle on the Fort Leavenworth course. This horse is a good, useful type of hunter, probably with a dash of Quarter Horse blood. He jumps quietly and in stride and would no doubt give any rider a comfortable day with hounds.

Photo by Guy Kassal

100. The Handy Hunter, in addition to meeting the ordinary hunter requirements of manners, pace, way of going, soundness and so on must be outstanding in such traits as ease of handling, obedience and agility. He must portray the type of animal that can hunt in trappy country and get himself out of trouble without excitement. Handy Hunter courses often require sharp turns, jumping out of an in-and-out or a pen, or the horse may be asked, after having been halted between the elements of the latter to turn sharply before taking the second. Handy Hunters are often required to pull up promptly at the sound of the horn when galloping between obstacles and the like. This is Ray Bates on Golden Joe placing in the above division at Fort Leavenworth.

Photo by Guy Kassal

101. Another popular class is for Pairs of Hunters. Sometimes the riders are required to ride tandem, as shown here, sometimes abreast, and sometimes the class rules stipulate that they do both, starting as tandems and changing formation at a predetermined point in the course. Generally speaking, hunter pairs are matched in color and size, though this is not obligatory. They are required to maintain a pace fast enough to keep up with hounds on a burning scent and the distance between riders, both on the flat and over jumps, must be a safe one. The lead horse in this picture is Napoleon, ridden by Whitney Smith. He is followed by The Joker with Miss Sally Leonard up.

Photo by Guy Kassal

102. At a different point on the Fort Leavenworth course contestants in the Pairs of Hunters class are required to jump abreast as demonstrated here by the brother and sister team Johnny and Amy Grasnick, on their matched bay hunters, Erin Moon and Junagi.

Photo by Guy Kassal

103. Colonel G. H. Wilson, Ret., former MFH of the Fort Leavenworth Hunt, is shown here on Gaturah as he and his companion, Mrs. Clifford Jones on Cha Cha, place first in a Pair class.

Photo by Guy Kassal

104. Classes for hunt teams, each team representing a different hunt club, are always spectacular. As with pairs, they may be asked to negotiate part of the course tandem style and the rest abreast. It is also common for the lead horse in the tandem formation to be asked, at the sound of the horn, to pull out, allow the other two members to pass and then come in at the rear. Ideally a hunt team is composed of a lightweight hunter, a middleweight and a heavyweight, the terms referring not to the horse's size but to his ability to carry 165 pounds, 185 pounds, and over 185 pounds respectively. The horses in this team, shown winning at Fort Leavenworth, do meet this requirement and present a beautiful picture as they take the obstacle exactly abreast. From left to right they are Hark McClain on Rusty (lightweight), Whitney Smith on Barbosa (middleweight) and Miss Ann Olsen on Gone Away, a beautiful heavyweight hunter. They are all members of the Fort Leavenworth Hunt.

Photo by Guy Kassal

Hunter Trials

Hunter Trials differ from ordinary hunter competitions in that the course is a great deal longer and gives the horse the opportunity of showing his ability under real field conditions. Quite often it leads across a road, requiring that the horse stop, walk on the surfaced road and pick up his pace promptly on the other side. When available, streams or even boggy places are used to show that the horse can handle himself well in trappy country. Hunter Trials are often an annual event in a hunt club's regular program. It is interesting to note that in England and in Ireland conformation hunters in horse show classes for that division are never asked to jump but are only shown on the flat. It is rare that such horses have ever hunted, since the country, especially in Ireland, is rough, and rare is the hunter of more than one season's experience that has not received a few honorable scars. In the United States such animals would be termed "suitable to become hunters," being judged as they are in England on conformation, manners and so on. However, in England and in Ireland the judging is much more thorough than in this country. The judges all wear riding kit and actually ride each horse that they consider for the ribbons. They can thus judge not only the animal's appearance but such things as mouth, flexibility and smoothness of gait, traits which are often improved on by the expert rider and not always easy to judge from on foot.

105. This is the fine Mile-Away Farms stallion Battlewick again, competing in the Moore County Hounds Hunter Trials with Mrs. W. O. Moss, first Whipper-in and Honorary Secretary, up.

Courtesy of Page Shamburger *Photo by Emerson Humphrey*

106. An unmatched team of hunters taken at the Goshen Hunt Hunter Trials are; left to right, **Golden Boy, Colonel** and **Born To Please.** Golden Boy has a fine show record. Under the tutelage of Mrs. Carol Russell he has won five championships and many ribbons. He has been shown as a Green Working Hunter, a Working Hunter, Amateur-Owner Hunter, English Pleasure Horse and Open Jumper. Mrs. Russell admits that he is more successful in the show ring than in the field, having a dislike for being required to bring up at the rear and, when allowed up front, a burning desire to outpace hounds. His breeding is unknown, but it is suspected that somewhere in his background is a touch of Tennessee Walker since, when excited, he tends to rack and click his teeth!

Courtesy of Mrs. Carol Russell *Photo by Norbert Behrendt*

Young Entry

Half the fun of showing, especially for the younger generation, is the necessary preparation. Just as the greatest value of the Olympic Games when they originated in Greece lay not in the results of the actual competition but in the fact that practically every qualified Greek youth underwent rigorous training; so, in the mind of this writer, the greatest value in showing for the young rider lies in the conditioning and training program of the horse which must be undertaken before either he or his rider are ready for competition. The junior whose parents buy him an outstanding show prospect and have it professionally trained may come home with more cups, but he will never know the satisfaction or acquire the practical knowledge in handling horses that is learned by the young pony clubber, the 4H member or the boy or girl who cares for and conditions a beloved horse or pony for local competition.

107. One of Mrs. Oliver's students gallops her Welsh-Thoroughbred B pony on the sandy shore. Walking up and down hills and galloping in sand are two ways of building muscle and wind.

Courtesy of Mrs. George T. Oliver

108. A trio of young people do the all-important braiding of an entry's mane and tail before going to the show. It is participating in activities such as this which makes a horseman and not just a rider. Notice the placid cooperation of the pony and the earnest concentration of the young handlers.

Courtesy of Mrs. George T. Oliver *Photo by M. C. Self*

109. High Jinx, a two-and-a-half-year-old grandson of Bull Lea, makes his initial appearance in the show ring. He is owned by Mrs. Charles A. Standish and ridden by Miss Cathy Standish. This young lady and her sister Marilyn (see Fig. 112), do much of the breaking, training and showing of the young stock. High Jinx, who matured at 18 hands, has been in many shows since his debut and has never been out of the ribbons.

Courtesy of Mrs. Charles A. Standish *Photo by Tarrance*

110. A winner's happy smile. This is Janie Olson and her pony Sultan. Janie has every right to be pleased, for she is the only Junior ever to have won the Junior High Point Championship, the Hunter Championship and the Overall Show Championship at the Fort Leavenworth Show.

Photo by Guy Kassal

111. Johnny Grasnick on Erin Moon competes in a Horsemanship Jumping (Equitation over Fences) class at Leavenworth. This capable young rider showed in the same show with his sister in the Pairs of Hunters class (see Fig. 102).

Photo by Guy Kassal

112. Marilyn Standish, age ten, on Plain Jane. Horse and rider are pony club members and as such learn not only how to ride but how to select, care for and train their mounts.

Courtesy of Mrs. Charles A. Standish

113. Juniors are not limited to showing in the junior division. This is Amy Grasnick competing in an open Working Hunter class at Fort Leavenworth on Junagi.

Photo by Guy Kassal

114. An outstanding and hard-to-beat combination in Southern California is ten-year-old Mary Jane Schy and her 12:3-hand pony **Mary Jane's Sugar.** Together they have won over 150 ribbons, including 25 blues and several championships. Sugar is a fifteen-year-old mare that jumps four feet with ease. She has won consistently with Mary aboard in Cross Country Hunter classes, Equitation, Jumper and Pleasure classes. She has shown successfully in such large shows as the Santa Barbara and the Palms Springs National shows as well as in other Western show rings. For variety, Mary Jane also competes in flat classes, both English and Western. Sugar received her early training from her former owner, Lisa Wolf. Mary Jane and her pony are currently in training under Bill Herring, well know for his many successful winners.

Courtesy of Ted H. Schy

115. Liz Jolly shows **GlenNant Oberon,** a registered Welsh pony by Mrs. Butler's popular stud Cusop Sheriff. The scene is the West Jersey Hospital Horse Show. Oberon is a consistent winner and has garnered several championships.

Courtesy of Mrs. Karl D. Butler *Photo by Tarrance*

116. The Tamarack Farm ponies are well known in the show ring. This is **Tamarack Fellowship,** a Welsh-Thoroughbred cross owned by Mrs. Oliver, with Kathy LaPort up. He is an exceptionally good large Pony Hunter type.

Courtesy of Mrs George T. Oliver   Photo by Colin H. Brearley

117. **Pojac Merlyn Myth** was Reserve Pony Hunter Hack for the State of Rhode Island in 1971, the championship going to another of Mrs. Oliver's ponies, Puck. Myth is shown here with Jennifer Curry up.

Courtesy of Mrs. George T. Oliver   Photo by Colin H. Brearley

118. **Pojac Elf** is being shown here as a three-year-old in 1971 by Pam Turner. He was sold before the season was out. Although he was shown only in Rhode Island, before being sold he was within ten points of being Reserve Champion of New England in the Pet Pony division. Too young to have started his career as a Pony Hunter, he will no doubt be heard from again, as he was gone to Maryland, the heart of the Pony Hunter country, both field and show.

Courtesy of Mrs. George T. Oliver   Photo by Colin H. Brearley

119. **Dasher,** bred in Maryland, is a gray Welsh gelding, exact breeding unknown. He is eight years old and his young rider, Caroline Francklyn, has been riding, hunting and showing him ever since she was seven. Dasher started making a name for himself in the shows at the age of three, has always been in the ribbons and has won many championships. More important, he is the ideal young rider's mount, combining the characteristics of pet pony, show pony, hunter, playmate and nurse. He can be trusted never to put an ear back or lift a foot in irritation no matter what goes on around him. He always jumps what's put before him, whether ridden by a neophyte who is still a "passenger" or by a capable young horseman. He permits "monkey drill," and Caroline can run from behind, vault on over his sturdy hindquarters, execute the "scissors," stand and jump around on his back and then step off his rump while Dasher stands patiently, not even needing to be held. In the hunt field he is equally reliable, sometimes in a trappy situation giving a lead to more timorous animals. Yet Dasher is no dog; he moves well and needs to be

120. **Step Ace,** #650726, is a five-year-old gray Welsh mare from Liseter Hall Farm. Her 1970 record includes three championships, four reserve championships, eleven firsts and twelve seconds. We see her here in a Pony Hunter class at the Devon (Pennsylvania) Horse Show. Notice how beautifully relaxed she is and how well she is using her head and neck over this rather unusually constructed spread jump.

Courtesy of Liseter Hall Farm *Photo by Budd*

---

steadied rather than pushed. Lucky is the youngster who acquires such a mount, and even were he not a winner at shows Dasher would still be worth his weight in gold!

Courtesy of Mrs. Reginald Francklyn *Photo by Tarrance*

121. **Liseter Blue Mist,** #5690, is another of Mrs. J. Austin du Pont's lovely Welsh ponies. With Betsy Buchanan up she is taking a post-and-rail in the National Pony Tryouts of 1963. Though she has cleared the obstacle with a foot or better to spare, she has done so as a hunting pony should: calmly, smoothly, in stride and with little apparent effort.

Courtesy of Liseter Hall Farm *Photo by Ernest L. Mauger*

122. The moment of truth: Holly Hopkins, riding Misty, cannot conceal her delight at receiving the coveted blue at the hands of Mrs. R. J. Olsen, head instructor at Fort Leavenworth. This was an equitation class, Hunter Seat. Though equitation classes, both those over fences and those on the flat, are judged on the rider's performance, the horse (or pony) has a great deal to do with who places. Some animals catch the judge's eye and make the rider look accomplished. Others affect the rider's performance adversely. The horse that has the habit of putting his ears back as he jumps, prejudices the judge, who may think that the rider's aids have been given too strongly. The horse with the rough trot makes the rider look as though he were working too hard. And so it goes. Horses merit large prices when they can make the rider look capable in such classes as the MacClay.

Photo by Guy Kassal

Steeplechases and Point-to-Points

In the early days before there were race tracks, steeplechases and point-to-points were held over natural country, each rider being allowed to pick his own route provided he reached and passed certain specified points before returning to the starting line. Hence the name "point-to-points." And since church steeples are easily seen from a distance, these were often chosen as the specified points and the term "steeplechase" also became popular. In Part I we saw photographs of English sporting prints depicting the type of country common in steeplechase courses of the early 1800s. By this time a cleared terrain was chosen for this competitions, though again the riders did not have to stick to a flagged course but could cross the natural ditches, bullfinches and gates wherever they chose. It was the popularity of competitions such as these that led to the importation of the three original Arabian stallions and thus brought into being the Thoroughbred horse. The following series of ten pictures were provided by *The Maryland Horse* and shows typical scenes from various races both over timber and brush.

123. A twelve-horse field over the first fence at the Trouble Maker Steeplechase at Fair Hill, Maryland. This three-mile timber race was won by Mrs. John B. Hannum's Bradford Meeting.

Photo by W. M. Ball

124. Night Dew and Haffaday take the sixteenth fence in the Maryland Grand National.

Photo by Winants Bros., Inc.

125. Whacker Jack, with Chase Hibbard up, leads over the fourth fence in the Elkridge Harford Point-to-Point.

Photo by W. M. Ball

126. A timber racer stands well back for a powerful takeoff. This is Good Trick in the Howard County Hounds Point-to-Point.

Photo by Winants Bros., Inc.

127. Only the bold deserve the prize. Here horse and rider both come a cropper at a solid obstacle. Fortunately, in the majority of such incidents neither would be hurt, and one can be sure that the second horse, apparently about to land on the fallen jockey, will neatly avoid him, since by nature a horse will never step on any strange object, be it the body of a fallen rider or an innocuous white mark on the road. This picture was taken at the My Lady's Manor Point-to-Point.

Photo by Winants Bros., Inc.

128. The brush course at Saratoga is one of the most beautiful. Note that the style of jumping brush is quite different from that of jumping timber. The brush horse, knowing that touching the top of the obstacle will do no harm, saves his energy and does not clear the obstacle with inches to spare.

Photo by Winants Bros., Inc.

129. The leading horse in this picture taken at Saratoga was aptly named Last Fence, for it was over that one that he bit the dust.

Photo by Winants Bros., Inc.

130. It was a misty day in Saratoga when this lovely shot was taken, and the field was still well bunched over the next-to-last fence. Appropriately enough, the winner was a horse named Tote 'Em Home.

Photo by Winants Bros., Inc.

131. A scene at the Maryland Hunt Cup Race with Early Earner leading, followed by Landing Party, Stutter Start and Prince Vims, the fifth horse having come to grief.

Photo by Winants Bros., Inc.

132. The second fence at the Maryland Hunt Cup. From left to right we see Arno, Island Stream, Morning Mac and Knockdown. The Maryland Hunt Cup is the most popular and most colorful of all the hunt races in the United States, being the American version of the English Grand National. To produce a

horse that will win it is the ambition of all breeders of hunters and steeplechase horses, and winning it brings fame not only to the breeder but to the owner, the rider and especially the horse. We feel it most fitting that this book should end with a scene from this classic race.

Photo by Winants Bros., Inc.

Index to Horses Pictured